GOLPHE DE VENISE

LES DE LA TURQUIE

dirigée par l...

17...

Bouches du Po
Comacchio
Ravenne
Rimini
Pola
Promontore
Fano
Foglia R.
Cesano R.
Siniagaglia
nuova

Urbin
S. Nutres
Marche d'Ancone
S. Angelo
S. Severino
Agubio
Mocera
Spoletti
Perouse
Todi
Rieti
Otricoli
Viterbe
Magliano
Castro
Tibre
Rome
Ostia
C. d'Antio
Terracina
R. de Garigliano
Tolturno R.
Capoue
Fundi
Sessa

Ancone
N. D. de Lorete
Fermo
Tronto R.
Teramo
Atri
Lanciane
Chieti
Popolo
Sulmona
Civitta
Burella
Lac de Celane
Aquila
Larina
Molise
Comte
Tragonara
Botano
Aquino
Voltuara
Benevente
Ariano
Capitanate
Broia
Naples
M. Vesuve
Conza
Nicenza
Basilicates
Herchonte
Sorrento
Amalfi
Salerno
Selo R.
C. de Licosa
Castella di Mare
della Bruca
Policastro
C. Palinure
G. de Policastro

Isles de Tremiti
Termoli
M. St. Ange
Manfredonia
Cantilari R.
Golphe de Manfredonia
Trani
T. Bari
Minerbino
Monte de Apeninne
Bari
Ostuni
Matera
Castell Tarente
Brindisi
Lecce
Branduno R.
Nardo
Otrante
Alessano
Golphe de Tarente

Palmirola
I. de Ponza
I. de Vento tieno
Ischia I.
Golphe de Naples
Capri I.

Meridien de Rome

Isles de Lipari
I. d'Ustica
Alicur
Felicur
Cephalu
Palerme
Monreal
Val di
SICILE
Mazara
Belice R.
Xaca
Girgente
C. d'Alicata

Panari
les Salines
Stromboli
I. de Lipari
Vulcano
Milazzo
Pietta
Messine
Taormina
Mt. Gibel
Saretta
Lentini
Val di Noto
Teranuova
Siracosa
Catania
C. degli Molini
Capo dell' Armi
C. Spartivento
Gieraci
Nicotera
Val de Mare
Regio
G. de S. Euphemie
L'Amantea
Cosenza
Martorano
Catanzaro
Izola
Squillace
Colphe de Squillace
C. Rizzuto
Brignano
Rossano
Cariati
S. Severina
C. delle Colonne
C. della nave
S. Marco
C. Trionto
C. de Bosito
C. de Lisse

NAPLES

Agri R.
Turci

To -
Madelyn -
People Who Eat
Well - Live Well

Donald Trump
Dec 23, 2006

Frank Grisanti

AND SONS

THE MAIN COURSE

Satisfying the Mid-South's Appetites for Fine Italian Cuisine for Four Generations

By

Frank Grisanti, Frank Grisanti, Jr. and Larkin Grisanti

with John M. Bailey

Written by:

Frank Grisanti, Frank Grisanti, Jr. and Larkin Grisanti with John M. Bailey, author of *Fine Dining Mississippi Style*, *Fine Dining Tennessee Style*, *Fine Dining Louisiana Style*, *Fine Dining Georgia Style* and *The Cupboard Cookbook*.

Cover Design by: Jim Hall

Text Design by: Maureen Fortune

Published by

TRADERY H·O·U·S·E

4650 Shelby Air Drive
Memphis, TN 38118

LCCN: 2005934637
ISBN: 1-879958-34-1

First Printing   2005   7500 books

WIMMER
COOKBOOKS

A CONSOLIDATED GRAPHICS COMPANY

800.548.2537   wimmerco.com

TABLE OF CONTENTS

Former New York City Mayor Rudolph Guilliani says hello at the National Restaurant Convention.

Larkin, Asher and Kimberly in Destin, Florida.

The kitchen at Caffe Grisanti.

DEDICATION:

This book has three dedications: my immediate family, my restaurant family and our loyal customers.

IMMEDIATE FAMILY:

I begin by first recognizing Ellen, my wife of 35 years, for her love, support and guidance. We have had a long ride together in the restaurant business, sometimes smooth, sometimes bumpy, but she has always stood beside me. Her view is, "Life is an adventure. Roll down the windows, let the wind hit you in the face and smell the fresh air." We have done that together.

I have two fine sons, Frank Jr. and Larkin. Never a day goes by that someone doesn't stop and tell me what fine young men they are and how blessed as a parent I am to have them working side by side with me. I appreciate their love and patience. I know its tough working with your father every day.

I have nothing but great things to say about my two daughters in law, Darby and Kimberly. They are loving wives and great mothers.

Many thanks to my grandparents Rinaldo and Mary Grisanti who instilled in me the true meaning of the phrase "work ethic" and my parents Francis and Elfo who taught us to accept people regardless of their race, color or creed. "In life judge people by their character and performance". To my father Elfo a special thanks. He was never recognized for the many things he did for his entire family during his lifetime. From him I learned humility. From "Big John" I learned how to treat and recognize people. He had a great talent for making people feel special even if they weren't important. That is a valuable lesson I learned from my uncle and former partner, "Big John". Thanks. To my sisters Dianne and Sharon (deceased) and brother Ronnie, thanks for all the great memories at 990 Dunlap, 135 Agnes Place, 1397 Central and 152 Grovedale. Also to Ronnie, continued success to you and your family in your endeavors.

RESTAURANT FAMILY:

To all the loyal employees who started out with me 26 years ago when I opened Caffe' Grisanti in the old Quality Inn Motel. Special praise must go to the following people who still work for me and are a major factor in our operation, Linda Huffman, Geraldine Hunt, Chef Michael Hunt, Chef Archie Wilder, John Cook, Gloria Lowry, Sean Pembroke, Rickey Martin and Brenda Webber. Their careers total 205 years of service to Frank Grisanti and family.

OUR LOYAL CUSTOMERS:

I started working at Grisanti's on Main when I was 13 years old. Some 49 years later I still have customers who talk about Main Street. We have third, fourth and fifth generations of families who are still our loyal customers. These people come from the Missouri Bootheel to Little Rock and from Jackson, Mississippi to the Tennessee River and all points in between. These people deserve special thanks for being so loyal to the Grisanti family for 97 years.

Frank Grisanti

THE GRISANTI FAMILY:
SERVING UP DREAMS FOR 96 YEARS!

Since 1909, the Grisanti family restaurants have served up a lot more than great pasta. Every dish has been richly seasoned with their own dreams...dreams that began in Lucca, near Bologna in northern Italy.

Frank Grisanti's grandfather, Rinaldo "Willie" Grisanti and brothers Ettore and Adolfo, along with two cousins left their village in 1909 and set out from their homeland for a journey to the American shores to start new lives and new adventures. Immigrants usually arrived at New York's Ellis Island or took the southern route and landed in the steamy ports of New Orleans. The fare was cheaper to dock in New Orleans so this is where the brothers and cousins first set foot on American soil.

The cousins, the Noe brothers, were successful farmers and storekeepers and chose to settle in the Mississippi Delta city of Clarksdale. Rinaldo decided to venture farther north to Memphis where the Fred Montesi family was known to give Italian immigrants jobs at their Liberty Cash grocery store. He ultimately became a barkeeper on Beale Street and soon went into the saloon business for himself.

Wedding bells rang in 1914 when Rinaldo took Mary Gusi as his bride and by 1930 the couple had added six children to the family. These included Elfo (Frank's father), John, Vivian, Arthur, Gloria and Jimmy. As the family grew, so did those dreams of the food and restaurant industry. The Grisantis found themselves face to face with an opportunity to build a legacy while introducing old country recipes to southern palates.

The first Grisanti family restaurant, rightly christened Willie's Place, opened in 1909 and was located at Main and Georgia streets in downtown Memphis. About five years later, the restaurant moved to 552 South Main, across from Central Station. It was now known as Grisanti's on Main and it is here that Frank began working at the age of 13 for his father, Elfo. Frank's own dreams of life as a chef and restaurateur took root here as well as his journey toward making them a reality. After a move to Linden and Walnut, Grisianti's returned to a Main Street address in 1954.

Following the Korean War, Frank's uncle, John Grisanti, joined the restaurant principals made up of Rinaldo, Mary and Elfo. He was lovingly known to friends, family and customers alike as "Big John". In the early 1960s the restaurant moved once more to the castle-like Ashlar Hall at 1397 Central Avenue. In 1962 John opened Grisanti's on Airways Boulevard and in 1970 Frank joined his uncle as a partner and remained there until 1976. Also in 1970, Frank married Ellen Larkin and began another partnership...this one lifelong.

Frank went on to manage restaurants in south Florida, including Le Dome of The Four Seasons, before being drawn back home to Memphis to open The Half Shell in 1983. During the next few years his professional credits grew to include his Executive Chef Certification through the American Culinary Federation and his Food Management Professional Certification from the National Restaurant Association Educational Foundation.

In 1986 Frank opened his own restaurant at the Quality Inn in East Memphis and within three years was ready for another big move to the current location. Frank Grisanti's Restaurant at the Embassy Suites Hotel on Shady Grove Road opened in November of 1989 and another Grisanti dream had come true. The same sense of adventure and longing that sent the earlier generation of the family to this country lives on in other Grisanti venues...three locations of their Bol a Pasta Restaurants are now in operation, including one which welcomes weary travelers to the Memphis International Airport.

Today, Frank Grisanti's menus are like a trip through old family scrapbooks. Signature dishes reflect the names and honor the memory of his father, Elfo, and grandmother Mary. The Elfo Special is a popular shrimp and pasta dish with delectable mushrooms and Miss Mary's Italian Salad is made with a previously secret recipe dressing and chunks of aromatic Gorgonzola cheese.

Is the dream still alive? As a reader and a cook, we'll let you decide. But just to give you a hint, Frank's sons, Larkin and Frank, Jr. are working alongside their father in the family business that now spans 96 years in the Memphis area.

Maybe the dreams are just getting underway.

ACKNOWLEDGEMENTS:

We would like to take this opportunity to thank the following people for their help during the creation of this book.

Kim Brukardt

Chris Glankler

Gail Glankler

Mike Gordon

Kimberly Grisanti

Charlie Long

Tom Mitchell

Gus Morris

Michael Prine

Terry Sesti

Arch Stewart

Ginger Wilkinson

Allen Gary Jr. (deceased)

Charlie Russo (deceased)

The front of house staff at Frank Grisanti's

The back of house staff at Frank Grisanti's

PROSCIUTTO WRAPPED SHRIMP WITH ROSEMARY BUTTER

Page 21

OYSTERS
ROCKEFELLER
Page 18

NANI'S SHRIMP
COCKTAIL
Page 25

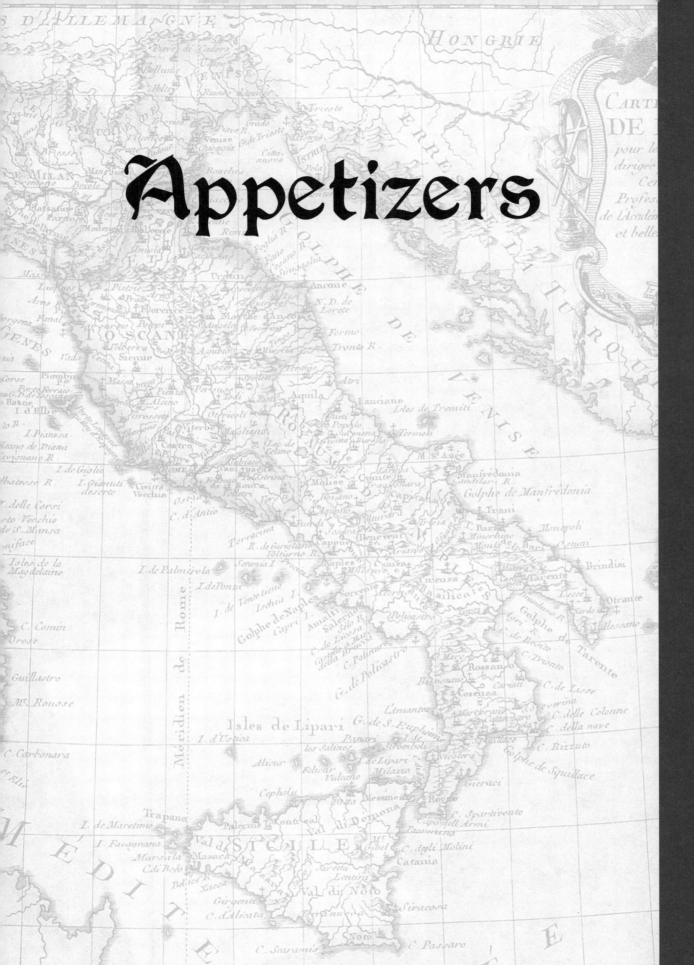

Appetizers

Frank and Ellen with former Secretary of State Colin Powell.

All dressed up for the visit from the 1951 Cotton Carnival royalty at the Catholic Club.

Preparing for the crowd at the Rendezvous at the Dixon picnic.

THE DIXON GALLERY AND GARDENS

4339 PARK AVENUE
MEMPHIS, TENNESSEE 38117

JOHN E. BUCHANAN, JR.
DIRECTOR

AC 901 - 761-5250
FAX 901 - 682-0943

June 3, 1992

Mr. Frank Grisanti
Frank Grisanti's at the Embassy Suites
1022 South Shady Grove
Brentwood, TN 37134

Dear Frank:

Wow! The credit goes to where it is due. Sunday's Rendezvous At The Dixon picnic was our most successful yet and it is thanks to you and the great efforts you put into making it the success that it was. With over 1,000 guests in attendance I can easily say it was the largest and most popular picnic to date.

As you may know a special thanks recognizing the picnic vendors will appear in the July members magazine. At this time we will officially thank all who made the picnic possible. Naturally, your name is on the top of the list; we could not have done it without you. Thank You!

Your enthusiasm for The Rendezvous Picnic and the Dixon is to be much admired. It is with support from friends such as yourself that the Dixon is constantly able to make all things possible.

Sincerely,

John

John E. Buchanan, Jr.
Director

cc: S. Herbert Rhea

JEB/ng

You are the greatest.
Thanks a million for all your help!

ANTIPASTO PLATTER

Serves 8 to 10

*When making this dish, we recommend that you use a large round platter.
Arrange the items in a spoke pattern. Be as colorful as you would like.*

1 head iceberg lettuce, chopped
2 (6-ounce) cans Albacore tuna, lightly crumbled
½ pound ham, thinly sliced
½ pound salami, thinly sliced
½ pound turkey, thinly sliced
½ pound Swiss cheese, thinly sliced
1 (8-ounce) can asparagus spears, drained
1 (4½-ounce) jar marinated mushrooms, drained
1 (6-ounce) jar marinated artichokes, drained
1 (4-ounce) jar whole pimentos, cut into strips
1 large handful of sliced black olives
Extra virgin olive oil
Red wine vinegar

Cover the bottom of the platter with the chopped lettuce. Place the crumbled tuna in the center of the platter. Roll each slice of ham, turkey, salami and Swiss cheese tightly. In a spoke pattern, place an asparagus spear with the tip pointing toward the tuna. Leave enough room to place the meats and cheese in between. Place the pimento strips just below the tuna and the mushrooms and artichokes above the meat and cheese combinations. Sprinkle a generous handful of sliced black olives all over the dish. Cover and keep cold until time to serve. When ready to serve, drizzle extra virgin olive oil and red wine vinegar over the antipasto.

FRIED GREEN TOMATOES
WITH CRABMEAT AND RÉMOULADE

Serves 4 to 6

FRIED GREEN TOMATOES:

1 cup cornmeal

1 cup flour

2 cups buttermilk

Kosher salt and fresh ground pepper

4 green tomatoes, cut into ½ inch slices, ends removed

½ cup vegetable oil

In a bowl, combine cornmeal and flour. Pour buttermilk into a separate bowl. Season each tomato slice with salt and pepper. Dip each slice into buttermilk and then into cornmeal mixture. In a cast-iron skillet over medium-high heat, add oil. Once oil is hot, add tomato slices and cook until golden brown on both sides, 3 to 4 minutes per side.

CRABMEAT:

3 tablespoons butter

1 pound lump crabmeat, picked for shells

¼ cup dry white wine

2 tablespoons fresh chopped parsley

Add butter to a sauté skillet over medium-high heat. Once the butter is hot, add crabmeat, wine and parsley. Sauté for 4 to 5 minutes until crabmeat is hot. Keep warm.

RÉMOULADE:

1½ cups mayonnaise

Juice of 1 lemon

½ medium red onion, diced

2 tablespoons capers, rinsed

2 tablespoons pickle relish

1 teaspoon chopped garlic

2 tablespoons fresh chopped parsley

2 dashes Tabasco sauce

2 dashes Worcestershire sauce

Combine all Rémoulade ingredients in a bowl and mix completely.

To plate the dish, place fried green tomatoes on a platter and top each with reserved crabmeat and a small dollop of Rémoulade. Garnish with fresh lemon wedges.

OYSTERS ROCKEFELLER

Serves 4

To ensure food safety, shop for farm-raised oysters.

12 large oysters on the half shell

1 cup butter

1 cup chopped celery

1 cup chopped white onion

½ cup chopped parsley

1 cup cooked spinach (fresh or frozen), well drained

1 cup seasoned breadcrumbs

2 tablespoons Herbsaint liqueur

3 tablespoons chopped cooked bacon

½ teaspoon salt

3 to 4 dashes Tabasco sauce

⅓ cup freshly grated Parmesan cheese

Rock salt

Lemon wedges for garnish

Preheat oven to 450 degrees. Melt butter in a saucepan over medium heat; add celery, onion and parsley and cook until tender, about 4 to 5 minutes. Add spinach, breadcrumbs, Herbsaint, bacon and seasonings, cook until mixture is hot. Transfer mixture to a food processor fitted with a fine blade and process for 1 minute. Top each oyster with the mixture, making sure entire oyster is covered, and sprinkle with Parmesan. Arrange oysters on a bed of rock salt and bake in oven for 6 to 8 minutes, until topping is hot. Transfer oysters to a serving platter and garnish with lemon wedges.

DEEP FRIED RICE AND CHEESE BALLS

Serves 6 to 8

This is a great use for leftover risotto; it makes a wonderful appetizer.
Be sure to fold the risotto in carefully so the rice will maintain its texture.

2 eggs
2 cups risotto
4 ounces mozzarella cheese, cut into ½ inch cubes
¾ cup seasoned breadcrumbs
Vegetable oil for frying
Freshly grated Parmesan cheese for garnish

Preheat oven to 200 degrees. Beat eggs with a fork. Add risotto and stir gently. Scoop up 1 tablespoon of the mixture; press a cube of mozzarella cheese in the middle and top with another scoop of the mixture. Press together and form a ball. Roll the ball in breadcrumbs and place on a plate lined with wax paper. Continue the process until all the mixture is used. It is best to refrigerate the balls for 30 minutes before frying. Heat oil in fryer to 375 degrees; fry the balls, 4 or 5 at a time for 5 minutes until golden brown. Transfer to a paper towel-lined plate and place in the oven to keep warm. To serve, place on a large platter and sprinkle with Parmesan cheese.

SPINACH DIP

Serves 10 to 12

This dip is great for raw vegetables.

3 (10-ounce) packages frozen chopped spinach

1 cup chopped green onion

2 cups sour cream

2 cups mayonnaise

2 teaspoons seasoned salt

1 teaspoon dried oregano

1 teaspoon dill

Juice of 1 lemon

Cook spinach as directed and drain well. In a mixing bowl, combine all other ingredients and mix well. Stir the spinach into the mixture and chill before serving.

GORGONZOLA STUFFED CELERY

Serves 8

1½ cups chunky blue cheese dressing

¾ cup crumbled Gorgonzola cheese

16 celery ribs

¼ cup sliced black olives

Fresh ground black pepper

Paprika

In a mixing bowl combine blue cheese dressing and Gorgonzola cheese. Wash celery stalks and trim the ends, leaves should remain intact. Stuff celery ribs with the cheese mixture and arrange on a platter. Top with olives and finish the dish with fresh ground black pepper and a pinch of paprika.

PROSCIUTTO WRAPPED SHRIMP
WITH ROSEMARY BUTTER

Serves 4

*We started doing this dish at the restaurant about two
years ago and it has been our best-selling appetizer ever since!*

16 jumbo shrimp, peeled, cleaned and cooked, tails on

8 slices prosciutto, cut in half

½ cup olive oil

4 tablespoons butter

1 tablespoon fresh rosemary leaves

1 tablespoon finely chopped fresh parsley for garnish

Lemon wedges for garnish

Begin by wrapping each shrimp with a slice of prosciutto. Cover them completely from just above the tail to the top of the shrimp. Pour olive oil in a nonstick skillet over medium heat. Place shrimp in skillet and sauté, but do shake the skillet. Allow the prosciutto to get crispy on both sides. Do this in two batches; adding more olive oil if needed. Once shrimp are finished, place them on a warm serving platter. In another skillet add butter and fresh rosemary; allow butter to melt until it is creamy. Pour butter mixture over shrimp. Garnish parsley and lemon wedges.

GRILLED OYSTERS SCAMPI STYLE

Serves 4

*This is a great dish to do for a backyard cookout.
You'll need to get the grill fired up for this one.*

12 oysters on the half shell, farm raised
¾ cup Garlic Butter (see page 60)
1 bunch parsley, chopped
Fresh grated Parmesan cheese
Lemon wedges for garnish

Lay out oysters, making sure to cut the muscle connected to the shell. Top each with a small amount of Garlic Butter, parsley and fresh grated Parmesan. Place oysters directly on the grill, shell side down. Cook for 4 to 6 minutes until butter begins to boil lightly. Remove oysters to serving platter, garnish with more fresh parsley and lemon wedges. Serve with some nice crusty bread so guests can mop up the Garlic Butter.

Butter dripping into the grill may result in a flare-up but this just contributes to the smoky flavor of the oysters!

BAKED BRIE WITH
HONEY AND TOASTED ALMONDS

Serves 10 to 12

This is one of my favorite appetizers. It is great for a cocktail party.

Butter or non-stick spray
1 (2½ pound) Brie wheel
1 cup honey
¼ pound sliced almonds, toasted
1 baguette, sliced on a bias, ½ inch thick, lightly toasted

Preheat oven to 375 degrees. Line a cookie sheet with foil and lightly grease with butter or non-stick spray. Place Brie in center of cookie sheet and bake for 5 to 6 minutes. Carefully remove Brie from the oven and top with honey and almonds. Return to oven for 2 to 3 minutes until honey is warmed thoroughly. Remove from oven and transfer to a large serving platter. Pour any excess honey from the pan over Brie. Arrange baguette slices around the Brie and serve.

BEEF CARPACCIO

Serves 6

The key ingredient to this dish is the meat itself.
Use only the highest quality filet mignon that you can find. A center or barrel cut is best.

1 (8-ounce) filet mignon
1 tablespoon extra virgin olive oil
¼ cup diced red onion
¼ cup capers, drained
Fresh shaved Parmesan cheese
½ fresh lemon, seeds removed

To prepare filet for easier slicing, wrap in plastic wrap and place in the freezer for 45 minutes to 1 hour. Using a very sharp straight-edged knife, slice filet into paper-thin slices. Lay slices in a single layer on a serving platter. Drizzle meat with olive oil and top with onion and capers. Finish by topping with shaves of Parmesan. Refrigerate dish for 30 minutes before serving. Garnish with lemon. Serve with peppered flatbread crackers.

SCAMPI STYLE SHRIMP

Serves 8

*This is a great dish when entertaining. The aroma of
the garlic butter is wonderful. Your guests will come running.*

2 pounds large shrimp
1 cup seasoned breadcrumbs
2 tablespoons olive oil
2 cloves of garlic, whole
2 tablespoons fresh chopped parsley
½ cup butter
Lemon wedges for garnish

Shell and devein shrimp, leaving tails on. Dredge shrimp in breadcrumbs and shake off any excess. In a sauté skillet over medium heat, add olive oil and garlic and sauté until garlic is golden brown. Remove garlic cloves and add shrimp to the skillet, cooking until firm. Add parsley and butter to the skillet and stir until butter is melted and coats shrimp. Transfer shirmp to a serving dish and garnish with lemon wedges.

BRUSCHETTA POMODORO

Serves 2

2 pounds ripe Roma tomatoes, diced
½ red onion, diced
2 tablespoons minced basil
1 baguette, sliced on a bias, ¾ inch thick (12 pieces)
3 tablespoons grated Parmesan cheese
1 teaspoon Italian seasoning
½ cup Gorgonzola cheese
3 tablespoons Miss Mary's Dressing (see page 44)

Preheat oven to broil. In a bowl, combine tomatoes, onion and basil. Set aside for 20 minutes. Arrange bread on a cookie sheet and toast lightly in oven. Turn all pieces over, top with Parmesan cheese and Italian seasoning and return to oven to lightly toast. Remove bread from oven and top with tomato mixture and Gorgonzola. Return to the oven once more until cheese is melted. Transfer to serving platter and drizzle with Miss Mary's Dressing.

NANI'S SHRIMP COCKTAIL

Serves 4

*My grandmother is from Massachusetts. She has made this dish as an appetizer
for as far back as I can remember. The cocktail sauce is the best that I have ever had.*

5 tablespoons mayonnaise
3½ tablespoons chili sauce
1 teaspoon fresh lemon juice
2 teaspoons prepared horseradish
½ teaspoon dry mustard
4 to 5 dashes of Tabasco sauce
20 medium-sized shrimp (peeled and cleaned with tails removed)
Oyster crackers

Mix mayonnaise and chili sauce together. The sauce should be a medium pink in color. Add lemon juice, horseradish, mustard and Tabasco to mayonnaise mixture and mix well. Place sauce in a covered container and refrigerate until ready to serve. In a large saucepan, bring 2 quarts of water to a boil. Add shrimp and cook until pink, about 3 to 4 minutes. Remove from water immediately, and allow to cool completely. Cut shrimp into bite-sized pieces and place in individual serving bowls. Pour sauce over shrimp and top with oyster crackers.

TOMATO BASIL PIE

Serves 6

1 (9-inch) pie shell
3 to 4 whole ripe tomatoes, sliced
1½ cups shredded mozzarella cheese
1½ tablespoons Italian seasoning
10 fresh basil leaves, shredded
2½ tablespoons olive oil
Kosher salt and fresh ground pepper

Preheat oven to 350 degrees. Prick the pie shell before baking to prevent bubbling. Place shell in the oven and cook for 5 minutes. When finished, remove shell and cool. Slice tomatoes and place them in a colander; sprinkle with salt and allow to drain. Combine cheese and Italian seasoning; Sprinkle half of the cheese mixture into the bottom of the shell. Place half of the tomatoes on top of the cheese and then add half of the shredded basil. Repeat layers. Drizzle olive oil over top of the pie. Season with salt and pepper. Bake at 350 degrees for 20 to 25 minutes. Remove pie and allow it to cool. Slice and serve.

Pre-baking the pie shell will help prevent it from becoming soggy.

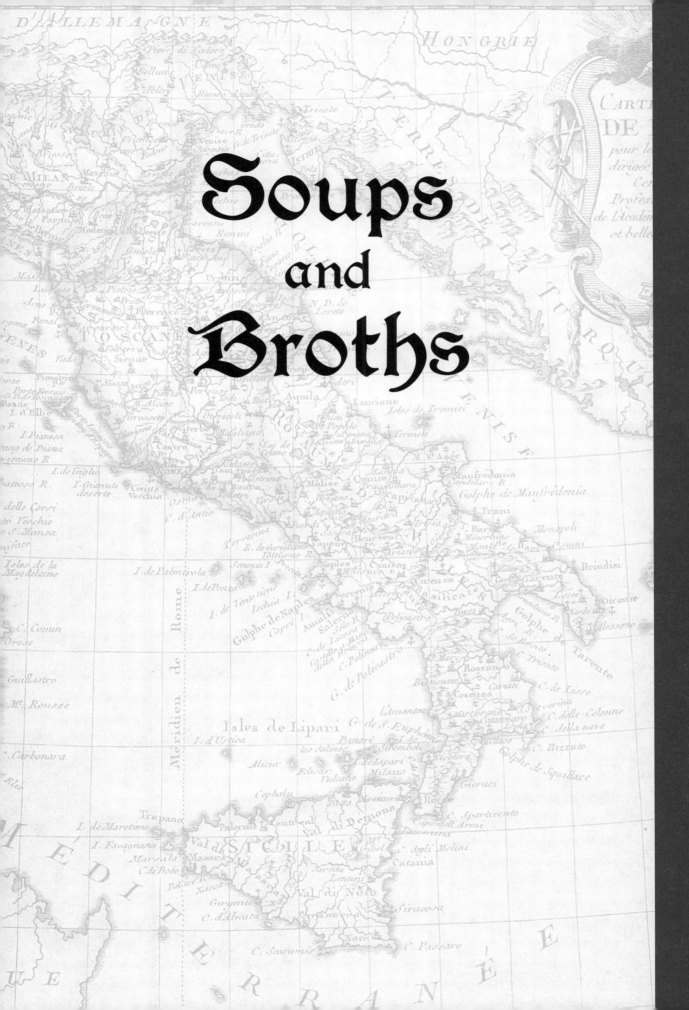

Soups and Broths

Frank (left) and Ronnie celebrate a festive occasion with Mom (Frances) and Dad (Elfo) at the famous Peabody Skyway.

Managers: Linda Huffman – 20 years,
Gloria Lowry – 17 years,
John Cook – 12 years.

Frank and his sisters, Sharon (left, deceased) and Dianne.

CABBAGE SOUP

Serves 4

¼ cup extra virgin olive oil
1 large yellow onion, diced
2 garlic cloves, minced
Fresh ground pepper
¼ pound pancetta, diced
1 head Savoy cabbage, chopped
2 quarts Chicken Broth (see page 35)
4 thick slices Tuscan bread
Freshly grated Parmesan cheese for garnish

Heat oil in a soup pot over medium-high heat. Add onion and garlic, season with fresh ground pepper. Sauté for 3 to 4 minutes until onion becomes translucent. Add pancetta and cook until it becomes crisp, 2 to 3 minutes. Add cabbage and stir until cabbage is well incorporated. Add Chicken Broth, reduce heat to medium-low and cook for 30 minutes. Place 1 slice of bread into each soup bowl. Ladle soup over bread and garnish with grated Parmesan cheese.

TOMATO BASIL SOUP

Serves 6

I like to use the vegetable broth with this dish.
I love the fresh garden flavor of the vegetables with the fresh basil.

1 tablespoon extra virgin olive oil

1 medium white onion, sliced

1 can peeled, crushed tomatoes

4 cups Vegetable Broth (see page 34)

Kosher salt and fresh ground pepper

½ cup chopped fresh basil leaves

1 cup heavy cream

In a sauté skillet over medium heat add olive oil and onion and cook for 5 to 6 minutes until onion softens. Add tomatoes, salt, pepper and Vegetable Broth. Bring to a boil, reduce heat to medium and allow to simmer for 10 to 12 minutes. Add fresh basil and heavy cream, incorporate well and remove from heat. With a stick blender, blend soup until smooth.

MINESTRONE SOUP

Serves 6 to 8

¼ cup extra virgin olive oil

2 garlic cloves, minced

1 medium red onion, diced

2 carrots, diced

½ cup frozen green peas

2 baking potatoes, diced

½ cup diced zucchini

½ cup diced yellow squash

½ cup sliced button mushrooms

½ cup green beans cut into ½ inch lengths

Kosher salt and fresh ground pepper to taste

5 cups Chicken Broth (see page 35)

1 cup peeled, seeded and chopped tomatoes

Freshly grated Parmesan cheese for garnish

In a large soup pot add oil, garlic, onion and carrots. Sauté over medium-high heat for 4 to 5 minutes until carrots begin to soften. Add all remaining vegetables, season with salt and pepper and sauté for another 2 to 3 minutes. Stir in Chicken Broth and tomatoes. Reduce heat to medium-low and cook for another 40 minutes. Taste and adjust seasoning. Garnish with grated Parmesan cheese.

FRENCH ONION SOUP

Serves 6

I love this soup! I like to use shredded mozzarella cheese instead of the traditional Gruyère.

2 tablespoons extra virgin olive oil

2 tablespoons butter

6 large white onions, thinly sliced

2 sprigs fresh thyme

Kosher salt and fresh ground pepper

½ cup dry sherry

8 cups Beef Broth (see page 36)

6 slices crusty bread, thick sliced

2½ cups shredded mozzarella cheese

Italian seasoning

In a heavy bottom pot over medium high heat add olive oil and butter. Add onion and thyme and season with salt and fresh ground pepper. Cook onion, stirring frequently, for 14 to 15 minutes. Add sherry and deglaze the pot, making sure to scrape the bottom of the pan well. Add Beef Broth and bring soup to a boil, about 6 to 8 minutes.

Preheat oven to 450 degrees. Place 6 ovenproof bowls on a cookie sheet. Ladle soup into each bowl, and top each with a thick slice of bread and shredded mozzarella cheese. Sprinkle with Italian seasoning. Place in oven and cook until cheese begins to bubble.

MAIN STREET BEEF STEW

Serves 6

1 cup olive oil

1 tablespoon chopped garlic

1 large white onion, diced

4 pounds stew meat, cubed

5 medium red potatoes, peeled and cubed

8 ounces tomato paste

1 cup water

Salt and fresh ground pepper

Add olive oil to a heavy bottom pot over medium heat. Add garlic and sauté until light brown. Place onion in pot and cook until it becomes translucent, (5 to 6 minutes). Add stew meat and potatoes; allow meat to brown on all sides. Add tomato paste, water, salt and pepper and stir stew until tomato paste is well incorporated. Reduce heat to medium-low and cook, covered, for 20 to 25 minutes.

VEGETABLE BROTH

Makes 3 quarts

3 tablespoons extra virgin olive oil

2 large white onions, chopped

3 carrots, chopped

3 celery stalks, chopped

1 cup button mushrooms, cut in half

4 garlic cloves

Kosher salt and fresh ground pepper

4 sprigs fresh parsley

4 quarts water

In a large sauté skillet over medium heat add oil, onion, carrots, celery, mushrooms and garlic. Season with salt and fresh ground pepper. Sauté for 6 to 7 minutes until vegetables begin to soften. Remove vegetables from skillet and add to a stockpot, along with parsley and water. Turn heat to medium-high and bring ingredients to a rolling boil. Reduce heat and allow broth to simmer for 30 minutes. Remove from heat and strain. If not using the broth immediately, pour it into a large bowl and refrigerate for up to 4 days. Remove hardened fat from broth before use.

CHICKEN BROTH

Makes 3 quarts

1 (3-pound) whole chicken

2 celery stalks, chopped

3 carrots, chopped

1 medium white onion, quartered

1 sprig thyme

1 fresh parsley sprig

3½ quarts water

Place all ingredients in a stockpot over medium heat. Allow broth to come to a gentle boil for 45 minutes. Reduce heat to low and skim the surface. Remove chicken from the pot when internal temperature reaches 160 degrees and set aside. Return to pot medium-low heat and allow broth to simmer for another 45 minutes. Remove from stove and strain. Season with salt and pepper to taste. If not using the broth immediately, pour it into a large bowl and refrigerate for up to 4 days. Remove hardened fat from broth before use.

BEEF BROTH

Makes 3 quarts

4 quarts water

3 pounds beef bones and trimmings

1 carrot, chopped

1 medium white onion, chopped

1 celery stalk, chopped

1 bay leaf

3 fresh parsley sprigs

6 whole black peppercorns

Salt and pepper

In a large stockpot over medium heat, add all ingredients. Bring broth to a rolling boil. Skim surface and reduce heat to medium-low and allow to simmer for 1 hour. Remove from stove and strain. Season with salt and pepper to taste. If not using the broth immediately, pour it into a large bowl and for up to 4 days. Remove hardened fat from broth before use.

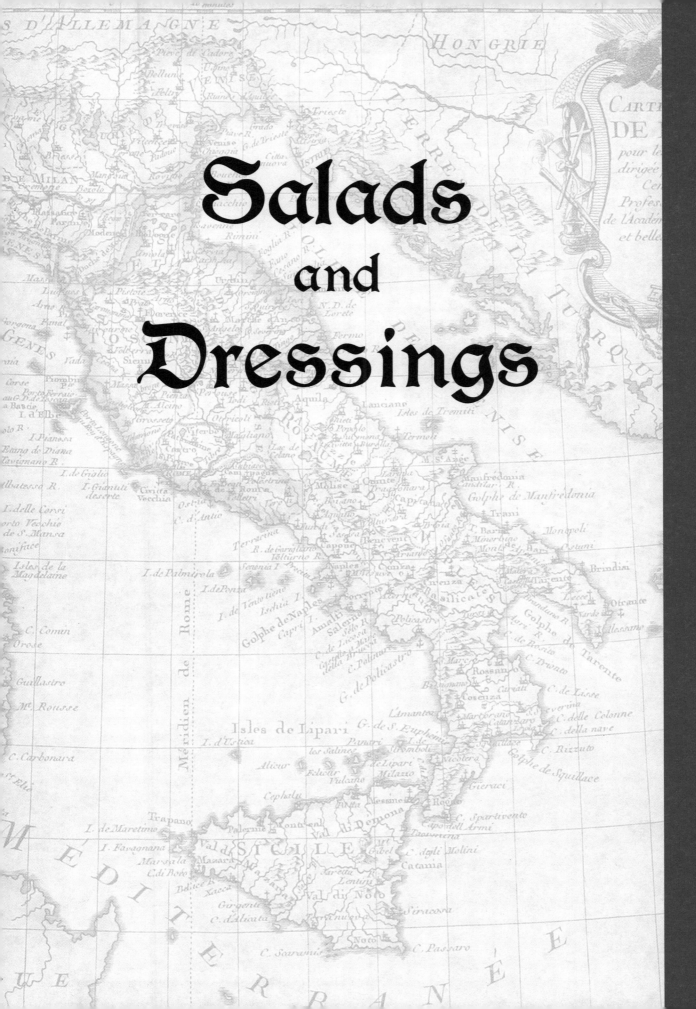

Salads
and
Dressings

Elfo's Liquor Store on Main.

City of Memphis

TENNESSEE

DR. WILLIE W. HERENTON
MAYOR

February 22, 2002

Mr. Frank Grisanti
Grisanti's Restaurant
1022 South Shady Grove Road
Memphis, TN 38120

Dear Frank:

Word is circulating around this great city of ours about a recent accomplishment that you should be very proud of. Please allow me to personally send my sincere **congratulations** to you for having been made a voting member on the National Board of Directors of the National Restaurant Association. They could not have elected a more worthy person.

Keep up the good work as I wish you the best.

Sincerely,

Willie W. Herenton

The Sign of Excellence

Here's Why

Frank Grisanti

VOTED #1 — Best Italian Restaurant By Memphis Magazine

VOTED #1 — Tennessee Restaurateur Of The Year

VOTED #1 — Wine Menu Design Tenn. Restaurant Assn.

CERTIFIED — Chef Frank Grisanti as a Food Management Professional by NRA

Dedicated to complete Customer Satisfaction

Serves only: Fresh Seafood & Certified Black Angus Beef

A Staff that renders courteous - efficient service

Frank Grisanti
Northern Italian Cuisine
EMBASSY SUITES HOTEL
1022 Shady Grove Rd. • 761-9462

Frank and Ellen with former President and Mrs. Bush at the National Restaurant Association Convention.

MISS MARY'S ITALIAN SALAD

Serves 4

2 heads iceberg lettuce
1 romaine heart
½ cup diced celery
½ cup diced white onion
½ cup diced green bell pepper
1 fresh tomato, cut into small wedges
¾ cup Miss Mary Mary's Italian Dressing (see page 44)
1 cup crumbled Gorgonzola cheese
4 Italian peppers for garnish

Tear or chop iceberg lettuce and romaine heart into medium-size pieces and combine with celery, onion, pepper, tomato and Italian Dressing. Hand toss. Separate salad into four equal portions and top each with crumbled Gorgonzola cheese. Garnish each salad with an Italian pepper.

GRILLED CAESAR SALAD

Serves 4

*This salad dish requires you to fire up the grill. Your friends
will love this one; you will be the only person on the block doing it.*

2 romaine hearts
4 tablespoons olive oil
½ cup Caesar Salad Dressing (see page 43)
¼ cup grated Parmesan cheese
1 cup Garlic Croutons (see page 60)
4 anchovy fillets

Prepare and heat grill. Split romaine hearts lengthwise, leaving cores attached. Drizzle olive oil over each half until well coated and place directly on grill. Cook for 15 to 20 seconds per side. Remove to a platter and dress with Caesar dressing, Parmesan, croutons and an anchovy fillet for each.

GRISANTI'S SPECIAL SALAD

½ cup sliced black olives

¼ pound diced Genoa salami

¼ pound diced cotto (cooked) ham

Prepare Miss Mary's Salad and divide onto four plates. Top with each of the above ingredients and Miss Mary's Italian Dressing (see page 44).

FRESH MOZZARELLA, TOMATO & BASIL

Serves 4

This is a classic Italian salad. I believe the true keys to this dish are ripe tomatoes and top quality mozzarella. We dress this salad with our Miss Mary's Italian Dressing, but you could use a simple combination of extra virgin olive oil and balsamic vinegar if you like.

4 ripe tomatoes, sliced ¼ inch thick

Salt and pepper to taste

Fresh basil leaves

4 fresh buffalo mozzarella balls, sliced ¼ inch thick

½ cup Miss Mary's Italian Dressing (see page 44)

Begin by laying the sliced tomatoes onto a serving platter. Add salt and pepper to taste. Layer each tomato slice with one basil leaf, followed by one slice of buffalo mozzarella. Drizzle the platter with Miss Mary's Dressing and more fresh ground black pepper.

To prevent it from drying out, don't remove the mozzarella from its packaging until ready to slice and serve it.

SUMMER SALAD

Serves 6

This is my favorite salad; it goes well with the Perfect New York Strip (see page 109).

4 ripe tomatoes, sliced in ½ inch slices
1 large Vidalia onion (or other sweet yellow onion), thinly sliced
2 medium cucumbers, sliced
1 cup crumbled Gorgonzola cheese
Kosher salt and fresh ground pepper
½ cup extra virgin olive oil
¼ cup red wine vinegar

Prepare salad on serving platter. Place sliced tomatoes on first, layer with onion, cucumbers and crumbled Gorgonzola cheese. Season with kosher salt and lots of fresh ground pepper. Add olive oil and red wine vinegar; refrigerate for at least 30 minutes before serving.

PANZANELLA

Serves 8

This is a classic Italian salad with many versions.

6 cups day old Italian bread, cut into 1 inch cubes
4 ripe tomatoes, cut into bite-size pieces
12 basil leaves, chopped
½ red onion, thinly sliced
2 tablespoons capers, rinsed
1 cup extra virgin olive oil
⅓ cup red wine vinegar
Kosher salt and fresh ground pepper

In a large serving bowl, combine bread, tomatoes, basil, onion and capers. In a separate bowl, whisk together oil, vinegar and seasonings to taste. Pour dressing over the salad and toss well. Refrigerate for at least 30 minutes before serving.

SPINACH SALAD WITH
ROASTED TOMATOES AND PANCETTA

Serves 4

*The preparation time for this salad is a little longer because you
must allow time for the tomatoes to cool. It is definitely worth the extra effort.*

16 cherry tomatoes
Extra virgin olive oil
Kosher salt and fresh ground pepper
¼ pound baby spinach
¼ pound pancetta, diced
½ cup Dijon Vinaigrette (see page 44)

Preheat oven to 375 degrees. Place tomatoes on a baking sheet and drizzle with extra virgin olive oil, kosher salt and fresh ground pepper. Place in oven and roast for 4 to 6 minutes, until skins begins to crack. Remove and cool to room temperature.

In a large skillet, sauté pancetta over medium heat until crisp. Remove and place on a paper towel lined plate to drain.

In a large salad bowl add spinach, pancetta and Dijon Vinaigrette. Lightly toss until evenly coated. Divide into serving bowls and garnish with roasted tomatoes.

WILD MIXED GREEN SALAD

Serves 4

*We have been doing this salad at the restaurant for about two years.
I first started doing it at our wine dinners and it has always gone over well.*

¼ pound wild mixed greens
4 tablespoons pine nuts, toasted
½ cup Gorgonzola cheese, crumbled
½ medium red onion, diced
8 cherry tomatoes, halved
½ cup Balsamic Vinaigrette (see page 44)

Place all salad ingredients into a large serving bowl. Add Balsamic Vinaigrette and lightly toss and serve.

GARLIC CROUTONS

*This is the best use for that great Italian sandwich loaf that
got stale before you could finish it. It makes all the difference in the world when
you take this extra step to make your own croutons. Your guests will really notice.*

½ loaf crusty Italian bread, cut into medium-sized cubes
4 tablespoons extra virgin olive oil
2 teaspoons garlic powder
2 teaspoons Italian seasoning
2 teaspoons Season All

Preheat oven to 400 degrees. Place bread into a medium-sized bowl. Add next 4 ingredients and toss well.
Place cubes in a single layer on a baking sheet and cook for 8 to 10 minutes until golden brown.

CAESAR DRESSING

Serves 8

1 egg
5 anchovy fillets, finely chopped
1 tablespoon Dijon mustard
1 tablespoon chopped garlic
Juice of ½ lemon
Dash of Tabasco sauce
Dash of Worcestershire sauce
¾ cup extra virgin olive oil
Kosher salt and fresh ground pepper

In a medium-sized wooden bowl, whisk egg, anchovy, mustard, garlic, lemon juice and Worcestershire and
Tabasco sauces. While whisking, slowly add olive oil until fully incorporated. Add salt and pepper to taste.

BALSAMIC VINAIGRETTE

Serves 6

*This is a quick and easy salad dressing.
It can also be used as a marinade for poultry, seafood and pork.*

¼ cup balsamic vinegar

1 teaspoon Dijon mustard

Pinch of kosher salt and fresh ground pepper

1 teaspoon chopped garlic

½ cup extra virgin olive oil

In a medium-sized bowl, combine first 4 ingredients and whisk together well. While continuing to whisk, add the olive oil slowly until all is incorporated.

DIJON VINAIGRETTE

Serves 6

2 teaspoons Dijon mustard

3 tablespoons red wine vinegar

Kosher salt and fresh ground pepper

½ cup extra virgin olive oil

In a medium bowl, whisk first 3 ingredients together well. While continuing to whisk, slowly add olive oil until all is incorporated.

MISS MARY'S ITALIAN DRESSING

Serves 8

1 cup extra virgin olive oil

½ cup red wine vinegar

2 teaspoons chopped garlic

2 teaspoons kosher salt

2 teaspoons coarse black pepper

Place ingredients in a bowl and whisk together well.

GRISANTI'S
SPECIAL SALAD
Page 40

GRILLED
CAESAR SALAD
Page 39

BEEF MANICOTTI
FILLING

Page 54

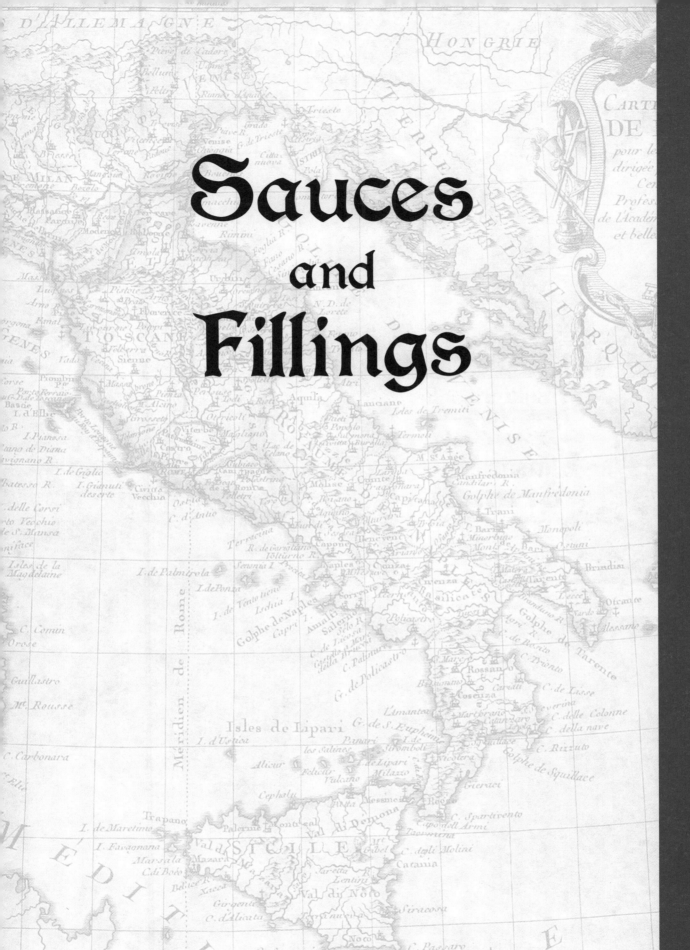

Sauces
and
Fillings

Day kitchen staff: Mike Hunt – 15 years, Rickey Martin – 9 years, Brenda Webber – 15 years, Archie Wilder – 20 years.

A very dinstinguished Elfo Grisanti.

Frank Grisanti

Sunday

Christmas

Brunch

Sunday, December 23
10:30 A.M.-2:30 P.M.
36 Traditional Items

$10⁹⁵ Reservations Suggested

Embassy Suites Hotel
1022 Shady Grove Road at Poplar   761-9462

Frank and his wife, Ellen, at Caffe Grisanti.

ITALIAN MEAT SAUCE

Makes 3 quarts

¼ cup extra virgin olive oil

5 pounds ground beef

1 pound Italian sausage

¼ cup chopped garlic

2 cups chopped yellow onion

2 cups chopped celery

2 cups canned mushrooms

1 tablespoon dry rosemary

2 bay leaves, crumbled

1 tablespoon dry sage

4 cups Chicken Broth (see page 35)

½ cup tomato paste

4½ cups peeled, crushed tomatoes

In a large stockpot over medium-high heat add oil, ground beef, Italian sausage and garlic; cook until meat is browned. Add vegetables and seasonings and cook until vegetables become soft, 10 to 12 minutes. Add broth, tomato paste and crushed tomatoes. Reduce heat to medium-low and allow sauce to cook for 2 hours. Stir frequently to prevent burning.

MARINARA SAUCE

Makes 3 quarts

½ cup extra virgin olive oil

1 medium yellow onion, diced

2 cloves garlic, chopped

1 celery stalk, diced

1 carrot, peeled and diced

¼ cup dry red wine

Kosher salt and fresh ground pepper

2 (32-ounce) cans crushed tomatoes

5 fresh basil leaves

2 bay leaves, crushed

4 tablespoons butter (optional)

In a heavy bottom pot over medium-high heat add oil, onion and garlic. Cook for 3 to 4 minutes until onion becomes translucent. Add celery, carrot, red wine, salt and pepper. Cook until wine evaporates, 6 to 8 minutes. Add tomatoes, basil and bay leaves; reduce heat to low and cook for 1 to 1½ hours until sauce thickens.

If the sauce tastes too acidic, add butter, 1 tablespoon at a time, to balance the sauce.

SEAFOOD CREAM SAUCE

Makes 2 cups

This is the sauce that we use for the Shrimp and Crabmeat Manicotti.

2 tablespoons butter

2 tablespoons flour

2 cups heavy cream

1 tablespoon seafood base

¼ cup dry sherry

In a small saucepan over medium heat, add butter. When butter has melted, add flour and mix together well, stirring constantly. Allow this mixture to cook for 2 to 3 minutes. Slowly begin adding heavy cream, continuing to whisk until all is added. Reduce heat to low and add the seafood base and sherry. Cook until sauce is smooth and coats the back of a spoon.

Seafood base is available at most supermarkets in the same area with bouillon cubes.

BEEF MANICOTTI FILLING

Makes 2 to 3 pounds

*Stuff this filling into cooked manicotti shells
and bake with meat sauce and mozzarella cheese.*

2 pounds ground beef

¼ pound Italian sausage

1 small yellow onion, finely chopped

1 garlic clove, minced

½ teaspoon salt

½ teaspoon dry oregano

¼ teaspoon fresh ground pepper

1 cup cooked spinach (fresh or frozen), drained and chopped

2 large eggs, lightly beaten

¼ cup Parmesan cheese

1 cup dry breadcrumbs

Sauté beef, sausage, onion, garlic and seasonings in a large, heavy saucepan over moderate heat until browned.
Remove excess fat. Reduce heat, add spinach, eggs, Parmesan and breadcrumbs and cook for 10 to 15 minutes.

BEEF LASAGNE FILLING

Makes 6 to 7 pounds

*This filling can be layered between cooked lasagne
sheets, topped with meat sauce and shredded mozzarella cheese.*

5 pounds lean ground beef

2 pounds Italian sausage

½ cup chopped garlic

¾ teaspoon dry oregano

¾ teaspoon kosher salt

¾ teaspoon white pepper

2 cups tomato purée

¾ cup canned mushroom stems and pieces

Sauté beef and sausage in a heavy bottom skillet over medium-high heat until browned. Remove excess fat. Add remaining ingredients, lower heat to medium and cook for 10 to 15 minutes.

ITALIAN MEATBALLS

*These are the perfect complement to our Italian Meat Sauce (page 51)
or traditional Marinara Sauce (page 52).*

1½ pounds lean ground beef

½ cup chopped onion

2 eggs, lightly beaten

½ cup dry breadcrumbs

1½ teaspoons dry oregano

1½ teaspoons dry basil

Pinch of salt

Fresh ground black pepper

2 tablespoons olive oil

In a large mixing bowl, combine ground beef, onion, eggs and breadcrumbs. Add oregano, basil, salt and pepper. Shape mixture into meatballs of desired size. In a heavy-bottom pot, add olive oil and allow it to get hot. Carefully drop meatballs into oil, one at a time; cook until browned on all sides, about 5-6 minutes. Cook meatballs in batches, being careful not to crowd the pot. Serve with pasta of choice and favorite sauce.

SHRIMP & CRABMEAT FILLING

Makes 1½ pounds

*This mixture can be stuffed into cooked manicotti shells, topped
with Seafood Cream Sauce (see page 53), sliced mozzarella cheese and baked.
It is also great to sauté with butter and white wine and serve over grilled fish.*

12 cleaned and cooked jumbo shrimp, chopped

1 teaspoon garlic powder

¼ cup fresh chopped parsley

Zest of ½ lemon

Pinch of white pepper

Pinch of salt

1 pound cooked lump crabmeat

Mix all ingredients well, carefully folding in crabmeat last so it will retain its texture.

PESTO

Makes about 2 cups

*Homemade pesto makes such a difference in the flavor of your dishes.
The fresh basil is so aromatic.*

1½ cups fresh basil leaves
½ cup grated Parmesan cheese
¼ cup pine nuts, toasted
1 garlic clove, crushed
Pinch of kosher salt
½ cup extra virgin olive oil

In a food processor, add basil, Parmesan cheese, pine nuts, garlic and salt. Pulse 4 or 5 times until a paste is formed. Scrape down sides of the processor. Begin to process again, slowly adding olive oil until it is all incorporated. Pesto can be refrigerated for 3 to 4 days or frozen for 2 to 3 months.

DEMI-GLACE SAUCE

Makes about 2 cups

¼ cup beef drippings

¼ cup diced celery

¼ cup diced onion

¼ cup diced carrot

4 button mushrooms, sliced

3 tablespoons flour

5 green peppercorns

5 cups Beef Broth (see page 36)

¼ cup dry red wine

In a large pot over medium-high heat, add drippings, celery, onion, carrot and mushrooms. Sauté for 3 to 4 minutes. Add flour and stir. Flour should begin to brown. Add peppercorns, Beef Broth and red wine; stir all ingredients well. Reduce heat to low and allow sauce to simmer until it reduces by half, about 1 hour. Strain into a clean pot and allow to cool.

ALFREDO SAUCE

Makes 4 cups

2 pints heavy cream
¾ stick butter
1½ cups grated Parmesan cheese
Fresh ground black pepper

In a sauté pan over medium-low heat add heavy cream. Add butter and allow to melt. Add Parmesan cheese and stir together well. Season with fresh ground black pepper. Cook until sauce is smooth and coats the back of a spoon.

PESTO CREAM

Serves 2

This is the sauce that we use to make the Farfalle Broadway.

2 cups Alfredo Sauce (above)
¼ cup Pesto (see page 57)

Blend Alfredo and Pesto together well and toss with your favorite pasta.

GARLIC CREAM

Serves 2

This is a very popular sauce at Bol a Pasta.
Most people order it on fettuccine pasta with grilled chicken on top.

1 cup Alfredo Sauce (above)
1 tablespoon Garlic Butter (see page 60)
1 teaspoon chopped garlic

Mix all ingredients well.

FRA DIABLO SAUCE

Serves 4

We use this spicy sauce for many pasta dishes.

4 cups Marinara Sauce (see page 52)
¾ cup Pesto (see page 57)
1 tablespoon chopped garlic
1 teaspoon crushed red pepper flakes

Combine all ingredients and stir together well.

GARLIC BUTTER

Makes 2 cups

Not only is this butter good for bread, it can be used to top grilled steaks or seafood.

1 pound butter, divided
½ teaspoon kosher salt
2 teaspoons chopped garlic
2 teaspoons garlic powder
4 teaspoons fresh chopped parsley
½ teaspoon white pepper

Partially melt half the butter over low heat. Cut remaining butter into cubes and add along with other ingredients. Whip mixture until smooth and creamy.

OLIO

Serves 2

This is a very light and fragrant sauce and is best served with angel hair pasta.

½ cup extra virgin olive oil
½ tablespoon chopped garlic
4 fresh basil leaves, chopped

Mix olive oil and garlic. Toss with hot cooked pasta and add basil. Basil will better retain its flavor and color if added immediately before serving.

CREAMY GORGONZOLA SAUCE

Serves 4

This sauce is best served with a heavy pasta such as, penne or rigatoni.
I also like to drizzle this sauce over sliced beef tenderloin.

1 cup Alfredo Sauce (see page 59)
½ cup crumbled Gorgonzola cheese
Fresh ground pepper
1 tablespoon grated Parmesan cheese

In a saucepan over medium heat add Alfredo Sauce and crumbled Gorgonzola cheese. Mix the ingredients together well. Cook until cheese has melted, 4 to 5 minutes. Remove from heat, add pepper and grated Parmesan cheese.

Illustration by Charles Tuthill

This part of the Grisanti family tree represents those connected with restaurants.

THE GRISANTI FOOD CHAIN

with
Frank Grisanti

In the Embassy Suites Hotel - 1022 Shady Grove Rd.

Fine Dining
7 nights a week. Featuring
Classic Pastas, Black Angus Beef,
Fresh Seafood and Fine Wines.

Daily Lunches
Monday thru Friday
Daily Entree Features plus
Salads and Traditional Pastas

And Our
Fabulous Sunday Brunch

Salads
Peel'em/Eat'em Shrimp
Oysters on the half shell
Macaroni Salad
Antipasto
Fresh Fruits and
Domestic Cheese Tray

Brunch Entrees
Eggs Benedict
Belgian Waffles
Cheese Grits
Crisp Bacon
Omelets made
to order

Lunch Entrees
Tenderloin of Beef
Carbonara
Shrimp Scampi
Veal Parmigiana
Au Gratin Potatoes
Beef Ravioli

Dessert Station
Chocolate Cheese Cake
Black Forest Cake
Pecan Pie
Assorted Pastries

Every Sunday
11 am - 2 pm
$14⁹⁵

Enjoy Memphis'
Greatest Brunch Value!

And For Special Occasions . . .
Our warm & casual party rooms for . . .
• Christmas Parties
• Wedding Events
• Award Banquets
• Retirement Parties
• Corporate Meetings
• Bar Mitzvahs
or any event of special significance

Here's a gift idea:
Frank Grisanti
Northern Italian Cuisine

GIFT CERTIFICATE GREAT GIFT!

GIFT AMOUNTING TO | HAPPY HOLIDAYS | DOLLARS
DATE 12/25/97 | GIFT FOR Mom & Dad | COMPLIMENTS OF The Kids | CER. NO. 0000 | $ 00.00

In the Embassy Suites • 1022 Shady Grove
Phone 901-761-9462 or www.frankgrisanti-embassy.com

Certificate of Recognition

FRANK GRISANTI'S RESTAURANT

IS RECOGNIZED FOR

14 YEARS

OF

PROVIDING HEALTHCARE
TO YOUR EMPLOYEES
THROUGH THE

CHURCH HEALTH CENTER'S

MEMPHIS Plan

Brenda Peterson
Assistant Director/MEMPHIS Plan

Dr. G. Scott Morris
Executive Director

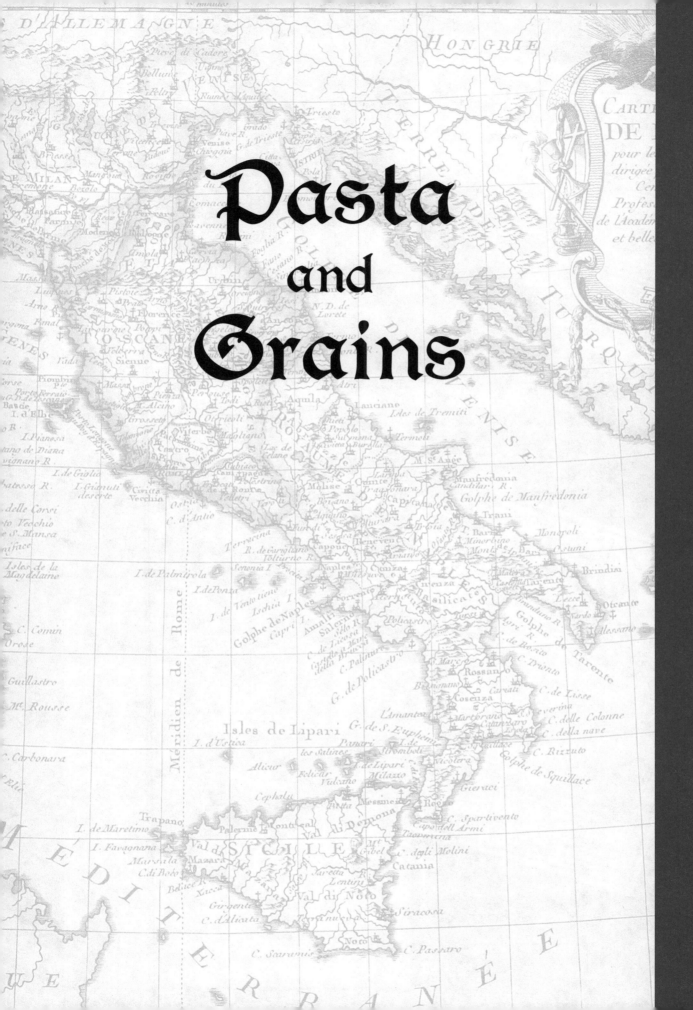

Pasta and Grains

MEMPHIS, WEDNESDAY, JULY 9, 1997

THE COMMERCIAL APPEAL

Bolla Pasta is so popular, Grisanti to go for seconds

If there's anyone who would like the idea of a big inexpensive bowl of pasta as much as Cordovans do, it's Germantownies.

Well, anyway.

Grisanti's first **Bolla Pasta** at 2200 N. Germantown Pkwy. in Cordova is doing so well he's opening a second in the Village Shops at Forest Hill, where the **Italian Oven** used to be.

The space will need some renovations, but Grisanti is aiming for an October opening.

The new Bolla Pasta will have the same menu and concept as the first, which is, as Grisanti described it, a "semi-upscale environment at a casual price."

Bolla Pasta caters to families who want a casual meal but still want to feel like they've gone out to eat.

Grisanti is also looking into opening a third Bolla Pasta in Jackson, Tenn.

Bol á Pasta in Cordova.

"Cut me a big piece, Elfo!"

SWEET SAUSAGE RAGU

Serves 2

We first started this dish about four years ago. It has been a local favorite ever since.

½ pound penne pasta

4 tablespoons extra virgin olive oil

1 pound mild Italian sausage

½ cup white wine

2 teaspoons chopped garlic

1 teaspoon Italian seasoning

1 teaspoon crushed red pepper flakes

1 cup Marinara Sauce (see page 52)

3 fresh basil leaves, chopped, for garnish

Freshly grated Parmesan cheese for garnish

Bring a large pot of water to a boil. Add pasta and a few pinches of kosher salt. Cook until tender, about 8 to 9 minutes. Drain and set aside. In a sauté skillet over medium-high heat add olive oil. Brown sausage, breaking it up into small pieces as it cooks. Add wine to the skillet, scraping up any brown bits from the bottom of the pan. Add garlic, Italian seasoning, red pepper and Marinara Sauce. Simmer at medium heat for about 4 minutes. Transfer penne pasta into skillet and mix together well. Divide the dish into two pasta bowls and garnish with fresh chopped basil and grated Parmesan cheese.

STORY OF ELFO SPECIAL

One Friday night many years ago, a customer came in to our Main Street location for dinner. He happened to be Catholic and at that time Catholics couldn't eat meat on Friday. He said he was craving a pasta dish yet all the pasta dishes we served contained meat. He asked my father Elfo if he would please prepare a pasta dish that didn't have meat. My father went into the kitchen and spontaneously created a dish that consisted of butter, garlic, fresh shrimp, mushrooms and spices. These ingredients were gently sautéed and ladeled over spaghetti noodles and topped with fresh Parmesan cheese. He presented it to the customer who absolutely loved the dish. The following Friday the same man returned. When approached by the waitress to take his order he told her he wanted that dish with the shrimp and mushrooms. When the waitress responded that we didn't have a dish like that on the menu, the customer told her that it was a special dish Elfo had made for him. Viola! The birth of the "Elfo Special"!

That recipe along with Grisanti's Italian Spinach, page 68, are probably two of the most published dishes to appear in various cookbooks across the Mid-South.

ELFO'S SPECIAL

Serves 2

Be sure to read the history of this very special menu item on the previous page.

Kosher salt
½ pound spaghetti pasta
4 tablespoons unsalted butter
2 teaspoons chopped garlic
5 medium mushrooms, sliced
12 jumbo shrimp, peeled and deveined, tails removed (cooked)
Salt and white pepper, pinch of each
1 tablespoon fresh chopped parsley for garnish

Bring a large pot of salted water to a boil. Add pasta and cook about 8 or 9 minutes, until pasta is tender, and drain. In a sauté skillet, melt butter over medium heat. Add garlic, mushrooms, shrimp and seasonings and sauté for about a minute and a half. Transfer pasta to the skillet and toss the dish a few times to combine ingredients. Divide pasta into two serving bowls and garnish with fresh chopped parsley.

ITALIAN SPINACH

Serves 2

1 box frozen chopped spinach (10 to 12 ounces)
3 tablespoons olive oil
1 garlic clove, minced
¼ teaspoon salt
¼ teaspoon white pepper
2 eggs
Freshly grated Parmesan cheese for garnish

Thaw spinach and squeeze out excess water; set aside. In a sauté skillet over medium heat, add olive oil and garlic. Cook until garlic is golden brown. Add spinach and seasonings, sauté for 3 to 4 minutes. Break in eggs and continue to sauté and stir until eggs are cooked and thoroughly mixed into the spinach. To serve, drain any excess oil and transfer to a serving platter. Sprinkle grated Parmesan cheese over the top.

PENNE POMODORO

Serves 2

This is a nice light dish, great for the summertime.

Kosher salt
½ pound penne pasta
4 tablespoons extra virgin olive oil
1 teaspoon chopped garlic
8 Kalamata olives, pits removed
½ cup oil packed sun-dried tomatoes, drained and roughly chopped
½ cup quartered artichoke hearts
¼ cup goat cheese for garnish

Bring a large pot of salted water to a boil. Add pasta and cook about 8 or 9 minutes, until pasta is tender, and drain. In a sauté skillet, add olive oil, garlic, olives, sun-dried tomatoes and artichoke hearts. Sauté for 3 or 4 minutes. Transfer pasta to the skillet and toss well. Divide pasta into two serving bowls and crumble the goat cheese over the top of each. Be sure the goat cheese is cold for this process as it is difficult to crumble at room temperature.

If desired, grilled chicken or shrimp may be added to the dish.

PENNE NATURALE

Serves 2

Kosher salt
½ pound penne pasta
¼ cup extra virgin olive oil
1 tablespoon butter
2 teaspoons chopped garlic
2 medium mushrooms, sliced
4 artichoke hearts, halved
4 pepperoncini peppers, diced
6 black olives, sliced
¼ cup white wine
Pinch crushed red pepper flakes

Bring a large pot of salted water to a boil. Add pasta and cook about 8 or 9 minutes, until pasta is tender, and drain. In sauté skillet over medium heat add olive oil, butter, garlic, mushrooms, artichoke hearts, peppers, olives, white wine and red pepper flakes. Sauté for 3 to 4 minutes. Add pasta and toss. Divide into two serving dishes and top with grilled chicken or shrimp, if desired.

PASTA PUTTANESCA

Serves 2

This is a very traditional Italian dish. Don't let the anchovies scare you.
They practically melt away when you sauté them and they add a light salty flavor to the dish.

Kosher salt
½ pound penne pasta
2 tablespoons olive oil
4 anchovy fillets, diced
2 teaspoons capers, drained
8 Kalamata olives, pitted
Pinch of crushed red pepper flakes
1 clove garlic, minced
1½ cups Marinara Sauce (see page 52)
Freshly grated Parmesan cheese for garnish

Bring a large pot of salted water to a boil. Add pasta and cook about 8 or 9 minutes, until pasta is tender, and drain. In sauté pan over medium heat, add olive oil and anchovy fillets; cook for 1 or 2 minutes. Stir in capers, olives, red pepper and garlic. Stir in Marinara Sauce and simmer for 3 to 4 more minutes. Add drained pasta and toss. Divide between two bowls and garnish with fresh grated Parmesan cheese.

FETTUCCINE ALFREDO
WITH PROSCUITTO AND BROCCOLI

Serves 4

Save clean-up time by using the same pot and water for both the broccoli and pasta!

Kosher salt
1 head broccoli
1 pound fettuccine pasta
2 cups Alfredo Sauce (see page 59)
6 slices proscuitto, torn into small pieces
Freshly grated Parmesan cheese for garnish

Bring a pot of salted water to a boil. Trim broccoli into small florets and drop them into boiling water; cook until tender. Remove broccoli from water and set aside. Add fettuccine to water and cook about 8 to 9 minutes. In a sauté pan over low heat, add Alfredo Sauce and bring to low boil. When pasta is finished, drain and add it to pan along with the broccoli. Toss well. Divide pasta among 4 serving bowls and top with proscuitto. Garnish with fresh Parmesan.

FETTUCCINE WITH MUSHROOMS

Serves 4

Kosher salt

1 pound fettuccine pasta

2 tablespoons extra virgin olive oil

1 medium white onion, diced

6 ounces wild mushrooms (porcini, oyster, portabella)

½ tablespoon fresh chopped parsley

¼ cup Beef Broth (see page 36)

2 tablespoons butter

Freshly grated Parmesan cheese for garnish

Bring a large pot of salted water to a boil. Add pasta and cook about 8 or 9 minutes, until pasta is tender, and drain. In sauté skillet over medium-high heat, add olive oil and onion. Cook until onion becomes translucent, 2 to 3 minutes. Add mushrooms, parsley and Beef Broth and cook until broth reduces by half. Turn heat off, add butter into the skillet and allow to melt. Toss fettuccine in mushroom sauce. Top with grated Parmesan cheese.

SEASHELL PASTA WITH
BUTTER, GREEN PEAS AND PARMESAN

Serves 4

This is a dish that I remember my mother cooking all the time.
It is quick and easy, but it has always been one of my favorites.

Kosher salt
1 pound seashell pasta
4 tablespoons butter
1 cup cooked green peas
Freshly grated Parmesan cheese for garnish

Bring a large pot of salted water to a boil. Add pasta and cook about 8 or 9 minutes, until pasta is tender, and drain. Melt butter in sauté skillet over medium heat. Add peas and sauté for 2 minutes. Reduce heat to low and add pasta. Toss well. Divide into 4 serving bowls and top each with a healthy amount of grated Parmesan.

SHRIMP SCAMPI

Serves 2

Kosher salt
½ pound fettuccine pasta
3 tablespoons butter
Zest of ½ lemon
½ cup dry white wine
6 black olives, sliced
12 jumbo shrimp, cleaned and cooked
1 fresh tomato, cut into wedges
2 cups Alfredo Sauce (see page 59)
Lemon wedges for garnish
Freshly chopped parsley for garnish

Bring a large pot of salted water to a boil. Add pasta and cook about 8 or 9 minutes, until pasta is tender, and drain. In a sauté pan over medium heat, place butter, lemon zest, wine and olives; cook 4 minutes. As sauce reduces, add shrimp, tomato and Alfredo Sauce and continue to cook until thick, about 3 minutes more. Divide pasta between two serving bowls and top with sauce and shrimp. Garnish with lemon wedge and parsley.

BAKED ZITI FRA DIABLO

Serves 4

This is a great family dish. You can even allow the kids to help out and have fun.
It is delicious the day you make it and maybe even better the next!

Kosher salt

1 pound penne pasta

½ cup Marinara Sauce (see page 52)

2 tablespoons Pesto (see page 57)

Crushed red pepper flakes, to taste

Olive oil

1 cup shredded mozzarella cheese

Freshly grated Parmesan cheese for garnish

Fresh chopped parsley for garnish

Preheat oven to 425 degrees. Bring a large pot of salted water to a boil. Add pasta and cook about 8 or 9 minutes, until pasta is tender, and drain. In a mixing bowl, combine Marinara Sauce, Pesto and crushed red pepper; mix well. Add pasta to sauce mixture and stir together until pasta is well coated. Lightly coat the bottom of an 8x8 oven safe baking dish with olive oil. Transfer pasta to the dish and smooth out the top. Cover entire dish with mozzarella. Bake for 8 to 10 minutes until bubbling and cheese is lightly brown. Garnish with plenty of Parmesan cheese and fresh chopped parsley.

LINGUINE WITH CLAMS

Serves 2

This dish may be done in one of two styles, red or white.
To make the red, add Marinara Sauce to the skillet before tossing the pasta.

Kosher salt
½ pound linguine pasta
½ cup olive oil
2 tablespoons dry white wine
1 teaspoon chopped garlic
Pinch of lemon zest
Salt and fresh ground pepper
1 teaspoon chopped parsley
10 whole baby clams
Pinch of crushed red pepper flakes
½ cup Marinara Sauce (optional) (see page 52)
Freshly chopped parsley for garnish

Bring a large pot of salted water to a boil. Add pasta and cook about 8 or 9 minutes, until pasta is tender, and drain. In a sauté pan over medium heat, add remaining ingredients and cook 3 to 4 minutes. (At this point, add Marinara for a red sauce.) Transfer pasta into the skillet and toss well. Divide pasta between two serving bowls and garnish with parsley.

SEAFOOD FRA DIABLO

Serves 2

This is a spicy one! Be sure to serve with a tall glass of ice water!

Kosher salt

½ pound fettuccine pasta

¼ cup extra virgin olive oil

2 cloves garlic, minced

¼ pound bay scallops

1 tablespoon unsalted butter

1½ cups Marinara Sauce (see page 52)

6 tablespoons Pesto (see page 57)

2 teaspoons crushed red pepper flakes

6 jumbo shrimp peeled and deveined, tail off (cooked)

¼ pound lump crabmeat, picked

Fresh chopped parsley for garnish

Bring a large pot of salted water to a boil. Add pasta and cook about 6 or 7 minutes, until pasta is tender, and drain. In a sauté skillet over medium heat, add oil, garlic, scallops and butter; cook 2 to 3 minutes. Stir in Marinara Sauce, Pesto, red pepper and shrimp and cook 2 to 3 minutes more. Add pasta and crabmeat last and toss gently so crabmeat remains in lumps. Transfer pasta to 2 serving bowls and garnish lightly with fresh chopped parsley.

MEDITERRANEAN SHRIMP WITH SHERRY

Serves 2

Kosher salt

½ pound angel hair pasta

2 tablespoons butter

1 tablespoon minced garlic

½ cup diced white onion

½ teaspoon white pepper

1 teaspoon Italian seasoning

½ pound medium-sized shrimp, peeled and deveined

4 button mushrooms, sliced

¼ cup diced black olives

1 fresh tomato, diced

6 tablespoons dry sherry

4 tablespoons heavy cream

Bring a large pot of salted water to a boil. Add pasta and cook about 3 or 4 minutes, until pasta is tender, and drain. In a large sauté skillet over medium heat add butter, garlic, onion, white pepper and Italian seasoning. Cook 4 to 5 minutes until onion becomes translucent. Add shrimp, mushrooms and olives and cook until shrimp become pink, 3 to 4 minutes. Add tomatoes and sherry; allow sherry to reduce by half. Add cream, turn heat to low and simmer until sauce is creamy. Toss the pasta in the sauce, combine well and serve.

FARFALLE BROADWAY

Serves 2

Kosher salt
1 pound farfalle (bowtie) pasta
2 cups Alfredo Sauce (see page 59)
¼ cup Pesto (see page 57)
1 roasted red pepper, diced
2 tablespoons pine nuts, toasted

Bring a large pot of salted water to a boil. Add pasta and cook about 8 or 9 minutes, until pasta is tender, and drain. In a sauté pan over medium heat, combine Alfredo Sauce, Pesto and red pepper and cook for 1 minute. Transfer pasta to sauté pan and toss well. Top with toasted pine nuts to serve.

FRANK'S SUNDAY RISOTTO

Serves 2 as a main dish; serves 4 as a side dish

There are two keys to successful making risotto. Never cover your pan and never stop stirring. This is a great dish to have in your repertoire.

2 tablespoons olive oil

2½ tablespoons unsalted butter, divided

½ cup minced white onion

1 cup uncooked Arborio rice

½ cup dry white wine

3 cups warm Chicken Broth (see page 35)

¼ cup grated Parmesan cheese

Kosher salt and ground black pepper

In a large, heavy-bottom pan over medium heat, sauté minced onion in olive oil and 1½ tablespoons of butter until translucent, about 3 to 4 minutes. Add rice and stir constantly for 2 to 3 minutes, or until well blended. Add wine and continue stirring until incorporated. Slowly stir in one ladle of Chicken Broth (approximately ½ cup), constantly stirring until all the broth is absorbed. Repeat this process one ladle at a time until all broth has been absorbed and the risotto has reached a creamy, yet al dente consistency, usually 22 to 25 minutes. Remove rice from heat and stir in remaining butter and Parmesan cheese. Season with salt and pepper to taste.

SEASONAL RISOTTO VARIATIONS:

SUMMER RISOTTO

Serves 2

Frank's Sunday Risotto (see page 81)
1 tablespoon olive oil
1 medium zucchini, minced
1 medium yellow crookneck squash, minced
Kosher salt and ground black pepper

Follow the preparation for Frank's Sunday Risotto. In a separate sauté pan over medium heat, sauté zucchini and squash in olive oil for 3 to 4 minutes until tender. When risotto has finished cooking, incorporate vegetables along with butter and Parmesan cheese, season with salt and pepper to taste and serve.

WINTER RISOTTO

Serves 2

Frank's Sunday Risotto (see page 81)
1 tablespoon olive oil
1 cup roughly chopped fresh, wild mushrooms (shiitake, oyster or any other combination)
½ cup frozen green peas, thawed
Kosher salt and ground black pepper
4 slices Applewood smoked bacon, cooked and crumbled

Follow the preparation for Frank's Sunday Risotto. In a separate sauté pan over medium heat, sauté mushrooms about 3 to 4 minutes. When risotto has finished cooking, incorporate mushrooms and peas along with remaining butter and Parmesan cheese. Season with salt and pepper to taste. To serve, divide between 2 serving dishes and top with crumbled bacon.

Any fragrant, thick sliced bacon may be substituted for the Applewood.

MR. WILLIE'S CHILI MAC

Serves 6 to 8

Kosher salt

1 pound rigatoni pasta

¼ cup olive oil

3 pounds ground beef

2 tablespoons chopped garlic

1 tablespoon chili powder

1 teaspoon crushed red pepper flakes

1 tablespoon ground cumin

Freshly grated Parmesan cheese for garnish

Bring a large pot of salted water to a boil. Add pasta and cook about 6 or 7 minutes, until pasta is tender, and drain. Place olive oil in a heavy bottom pot over medium heat. Add ground beef and as the meat begins to brown, add garlic, chili powder, red pepper flakes and cumin. Stir the seasonings into the meat well. Continue to cook over medium heat until ground beef is thoroughly cooked. Toss pasta into meat mixture and serve immediately. Top each serving with grated Parmesan cheese.

GRILLED POLENTA SQUARES
WITH SAUSAGE RAGU

Serves 4

1 teaspoon kosher salt

2 cups polenta

2 tablespoons butter

Sweet Sausage Ragu (see page 65)

Freshly grated Parmesan cheese for garnish

Bring 6 cups of water to a boil and season with kosher salt. Reduce heat to medium and slowly add polenta, stirring constantly. Cook for 25 to 30 minutes until polenta begins to thicken and pull away from the sides of the pot. When polenta is finished, add butter and pour into a greased 9x13 dish and allow to cool. In a separate skillet, prepare the Sweet Sausage Ragu and keep warm over low heat. Heat grill according to manufacturer's instructions. Once the polenta is cool, cut into 3x3 squares and place on grill. Grill polenta for 3 to 4 minutes per side. To serve, place the polenta squares on a serving platter and top with Sweet Sausage Ragu and grated Parmesan.

SOFT POLENTA
WITH GORGONZOLA CHEESE

Serves 8

1 teaspoon kosher salt

1½ cups polenta

2 tablespoons butter

½ cup crumbled Gorgonzola cheese

Bring 6 cups of water to a boil and season with kosher salt. Reduce heat to medium and slowly add polenta, stirring constantly. Cook for 25 to 30 minutes until polenta begins to thicken and pull away from the sides of the pot. Remove pot from heat and stir in butter and Gorgonzola cheese. Serve immediately.

EGGPLANT PARMIGIANA

Serves 6

This recipe is a great accompaniment to pasta.

2 cups olive oil, divided

1 clove garlic, finely minced

1 cup chopped onion

5 cups drained and chopped Italian tomatoes, fresh or canned

½ teaspoon dried basil

Salt and freshly ground black pepper to taste

2 tablespoons flour

1 egg, beaten

2 eggplants, peeled and cut into ⅓ inch slices

1 cup grated Parmesan cheese

½ cup diced mozzarella cheese

Butter

Heat ¼ cup olive oil in a heavy skillet. Add garlic and onion and sauté until onion is transparent. Add tomatoes, basil, salt and pepper and cook, stirring occasionally, 30 minutes. Preheat oven to 350 degrees. Combine flour, egg and ¼ teaspoon salt. Dip eggplant slices in batter and fry in remaining oil until lightly browned on both sides. Place alternate layers of eggplant, sauce and cheeses in a large casserole. Dot with butter and bake 30 minutes.

QUALITY INN

CAFFE GRISANTI
THANK YOU

RECIPE FOR SUCCESS

Name: Frank Grisanti, 48
Restaurant: Frank Grisanti's Restaurant, 1022 Shady Grove in the Embassy Suites
Background/education: I started with the family when I was about 13, with my father, Elfo, and my grandfather, Willie. I got my basic training with them. I'm certified as an executive chef by the American Culinary Federation and earned through the Michigan State University School of Hotel Management in nutrition and sanitation.
Professional experience: John (Frank's uncle "Big John" Grisanti) and I were partners at Lamar and Airways for about 10 years. I left Memphis and was in Fort Lauderdale and Miami for about seven years at three restaurants: La Dome, Gibby's Steakhouse and Cafe Ambience. I returned to Memphis in 1986 and opened the restaurant at the Quality Inn. We moved here (the Embassy Suites) in 1989.
Dining at home: Ellen and I love to cook at home. We spend a lot of time cooking on Sunday, enjoying a bottle of wine and testing recipes.
Dining out: We like everybody's barbecue. Houston's on Sunday after church. Late-night, we usually go to the Belmont. It's Chez Philippo when we put on the coat and tie.
Most essential piece of equipment: The senses of the chef, sight and smell, are more important than any piece of equipment.
Who influenced you? I would say my grandfather and my dad in my early years. Later, in Florida, Paul Bergeron, the chef I worked with in Florida. In Memphis it was all meatballs and spaghetti, that was all that was around. Working with Paul in a metropolitan area sent me back to Memphis with different ideas.
A trick of the trade: Keep it simple, keep it basic. Concentrate on a couple of dishes you know you can do well.

TRAVELHOST

SPOTLIGHT: FRANK GRISANTI'S

Memphians who rave about the fine cuisine of Chef Frank Grisanti now have something else to delight in—Chef Grisanti has moved his restaurant to the beautiful surroundings of the Embassy Suites Hotel. The casually elegant restaurant in Memphis' newest fine hotel provides diners with relaxed, intimate quarters in which to enjoy Frank Grisanti's superb Northern Italian dishes.

The decor of dark wood and rich burgundy is perfect for small dinners or large parties. With canopied tables at the restaurant entrance, casual diners can enjoy lunch or brunch in the charming atrium of the hotel.

Good food and great restaurants are a Grisanti family tradition. Frank's grandparents, Elfo and Mary, operated a well-known eatery in Memphis, and you'll find tributes to them both on Frank's menu. Grisanti is continuing the tradition with his son, Frank, Jr., who welcomes diners and assures smooth service.

In true Italian tradition, the menu offers a wide variety. There are the well-known veal dishes, classic pastas, steaks, chicken and seafood. Pasta for the cannelloni and manicotti dishes are made on the premises; all others are imported from Italy. The menu features combination dinners so you can sample several items.

We started our evening with some wonderful appetizers—toasted ravioli, baked brie with pesto mussels a la Romana and oysters Rockefeller. From the beginning we knew that this would be a special meal! The brie was beautifully presented with pimento topping the pesto. The cheese was warm and soft; the pesto was flavorful. Served in a creamy garlic-butter sauce, the mussels were spinach flavored with anise and other herbs topped the oysters Rockefeller. They were a real treat! And everybody loved the accompanying marinara sauce.

The entrees were superb. King Salmon Filet was served with Pasta Primavera. The 10-ounce filet of salmon was well prepared, topped with fresh broccoli and tomatoes that had been seasoned with a touch of curry. The angel hair pasta in the dish was cooked to perfection.

Seafood Fettucine, another entree, featured jumbo Gulf shrimp, bay scallops and fresh mushrooms blended in Alfredo sauce. Again, the pasta was cooked to perfection and the portions of seafood were generous and well seasoned. Veal Piccate presented two large slices of tender veal dipped in beaten egg, sautéed in butter, and topped with a fresh lemon and parsley butter. Veal Marsala presented the meat sautéed in oil and butter and served in a sauce of sweet Marsala wine.

Cannelloni Besamela featured handmade pasta rolled very thin and filled with mushrooms in a creamy bechamel sauce—delicious! Manicotti Carne offered tubular pasta stuffed with beef, veal and a special spinach filling. These dishes are not to be missed!

To complete the evening we ordered two desserts, chocolate cheesecake and bananas Foster. The cheesecake, served in a pastry crust, was wonderfully rich with the intense flavor of unadulterated chocolate. Bananas Foster was prepared tableside by our talented waiter. The resulting dish was delicious as well as memorable—a great way to end a wonderful dining experience!

Grisanti, Sr. is a Certified Chief Executive Chef, as designated by the American Culinary Federation, and the menu speaks to his experience and expertise. The new facilities also allow Chef Grisanti to cater to whatever party need you have, from wedding reception to bar mitzvah, cocktail party for 300 or a seated dinner for 225.

Frank Grisanti's is located just off the lobby of The Embassy Suites Hotel at 1022 Shady Grove Road at Poplar, just east of Poplar and I-240, behind the Regalia Center. They are open daily for lunch and dinner. For reservations call 761-9462.

RESTAURANTS

Zinnie's Mid-Town Restaurant and gathering place. Top choice steaks, fresh seafood and a variety of sandwiches. Lunch and dinner. All the crab legs you can eat Sunday night ($12.95.) Watch scheduled sports events on our Big Screen TV. Located at 1718 Madison Ave., 274-7101. Map C-4.

The Spaghetti Warehouse Located in a warehouse attractively decorated with old signs, old furniture and ceiling fans. Menu includes spaghetti and a selection of sauces, chicken and veal parmigiana and baked lasagne. Located at 40 West Huling, 521-0907. Map downtown.

Jim's Place East In wooded surroundings. Features steaks, seafood, Greek specialties, extensive wine list. Closed for lunch Sat. and all day Sun. Located at 5560 Shelby Oaks, 388-7200. Major credit cards. Map F-2.

Trumpets Restaurant "Memphis' most famous buffet" features fresh foods prepared in traditional fashion. Dinner specials and full service menu. Breakfast/lunch 6 a.m.-2 p.m.; dinner 5:30-10 p.m.; Fri. 11 a.m.-11 p.m. Located in the Radisson Inn, S.W. Airport, 1471 East Brooks Road, 332-3500. Map C-6.

Anderton's A Memphis tradition for over 40 years. Serving the finest fresh Gulf Coast seafood and oysters on the half shell year-round. Prime charcoal broiled steaks. Open Mon.-Thurs. 11 a.m.-10 p.m.; Fri. 11 a.m.-11 p.m.; Sat. 4-11 p.m. Closed Sun. Cocktail lounge. At 1901 Madison Ave., 726-4010. Map C-4.

The Bar-B-Q Shop features full array of pork, beef and Polish sausage sandwiches and plates. Try their Bar-B-Q spaghetti. Serving the same recipe for 20 years, "Best Bar-B-Q sandwich in Memphis." Lunch specials, Mon.-Fri. 11 a.m.-2 p.m. Children's menu. Open for lunch and dinner. Major credit cards. Located at 1782 Madison Ave., 272-1277. Map C-4.

Ruth's Chris Steak House Featuring only U.S. prime corn-fed beef, also excellent fresh seafood, and lobster. Lounge opens 5 p.m.; dinner 5-11 p.m. Mon.-Sat.; 5-9:30 p.m. Sun. Major credit cards. 5858 Ridgeway Center Parkway, near Omni Hotel. Reservations suggested. Call 901-761-0055. Map E-4.

Anthony's Serving French, Italian and Mediterranean cuisine. Casual dining in an elegant, intimate setting. Sauces, breads, desserts, pasta are prepared on premises from the freshest ingredients by Chef Gene Bjorklund. Full bar; excellent wine list. Reservations suggested. Open Mon.-Thurs. 5:30-9:30 p.m.; Fri. and Sat. 5:30-10:30 p.m. Located at 5469 Poplar Avenue/I-240. Call 683-2990. Major credit cards accepted. Map E-4.

T-Bones Steaks "better than your back yard." Also seafood, chicken. Casual dining. Children's menu. Lunch specials—try their '50s burger. Open for lunch and dinner every day. Happy hour every day from noon-6 p.m. Located at 5355 Poplar Ave./I-240. Major credit cards accepted. Phone 763-BONE. Map E-4.

Frank Grisanti, Sr. Elected by TRA

Frank Grisanti, Sr. President of Foodline Services Inc., Frank Grisanti's Embassy Suites Restaurant and Grisanti's Bolla' Pasta Restaurants has been elected President of the Tennessee Restaurant Association.

Mr. Grisanti's election marks the first time in 20 years that a Memphian has held that position.

SHRIMP SCAMPI
Page 75

ELFO'S SPECIAL
Page 67

SWEET
SAUSAGE RAGU
Page 65

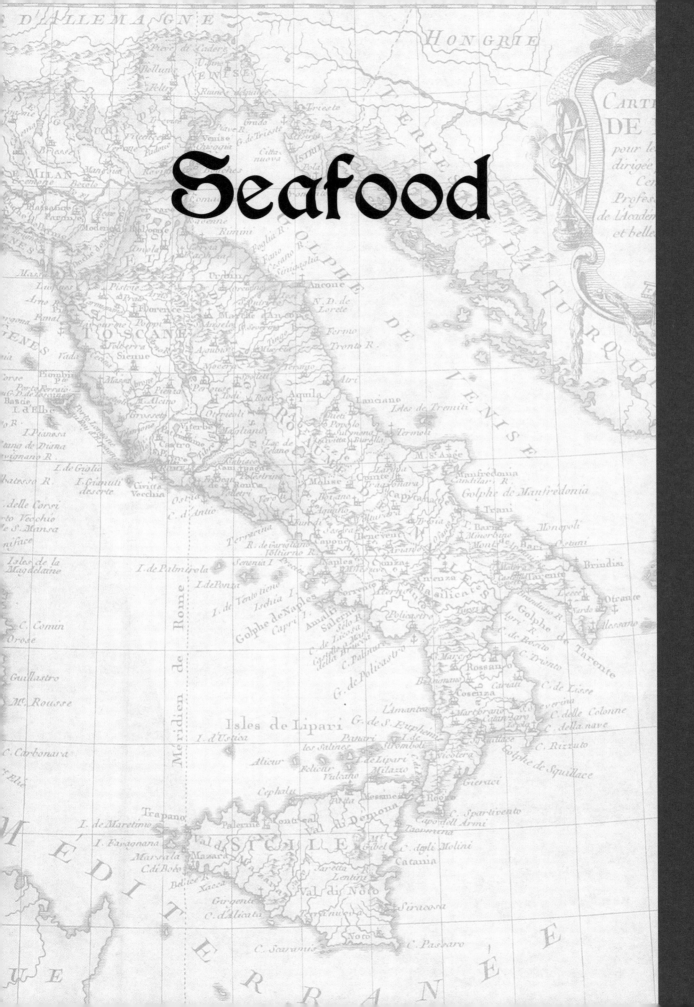

Seafood

Frank, Sr., Frank, Jr., Darby, Ellen, Larkin and Kimberly at Larkin and Kimberly's Reheasal Dinner, 2000

Frank Grisanti's gets a great review by Memphis Magazine's Tom Martin.

Big John, Elfo, Mary and Willie at Grisanti's on Main.

SALMON BRUNO

Serves 2

2 tablespoons olive oil
2 (8-ounce) salmon fillets
Kosher salt and fresh ground pepper
¼ cup dark brown sugar
2 tablespoons butter
Juice of ½ lemon
4 cups fresh baby spinach, stems removed
¼ cup goat cheese

Preheat oven to 400 degrees. Heat olive oil in a sauté skillet over medium-high heat. Season salmon fillets with salt and fresh ground pepper. Sauté for 2 minutes, flesh side down, and then flip to the skin side and sauté for another minute. Drain oil from skillet. Top each fillet with brown sugar and transfer skillet to oven for 3 to 4 minutes. In separate skillet, melt butter over medium-high heat and add lemon juice. Sauté spinach in lemon butter mixture until wilted. Top each fillet with warm wilted spinach and goat cheese.

PESTO AND PARMESAN CRUSTED SALMON

Serves 2

3 tablespoons olive oil
2 (8-ounce) salmon fillets
Kosher salt and fresh ground pepper
¼ cup Pesto (see page 57)
2 tablespoons Parmesan cheese
½ teaspoon toasted pine nuts

Preheat oven to 400 degrees. Heat olive oil in a sauté skillet over medium high heat. Season salmon fillets with kosher salt and fresh ground pepper. Sauté for 2 minutes, flesh side down and then flip to the skin side and sauté for another minute. In a small bowl, combine the Pesto and Parmesan. Top each fillet with the Pesto and Parmesan mixture and place sauté skillet in oven for 2 minutes. Remove from oven and transfer to serving plates and top each with toasted pine nuts.

BLACKENED GROUPER

Serves 2

This is a great dish that we have been doing at the restaurant for about 15 years. We recommend serving it with our Elfo Special Pasta (see page 66). This recipe does require a good cast iron skillet.

2 tablespoons butter, divided
2 (8-ounce) grouper fillets
Cajun blackened seasoning
Lemon wedges for garnish

Heat skillet over high heat. In a microwave, melt 1 tablespoon of butter and liberally brush over fillets. Heavily coat each fillet with Cajun seasoning. Lay the grouper fillets in the cast iron skillet. Cook the fish 4 to 5 minutes on each side until well blackened. Melt remaining butter and drizzle over fish just prior to serving. Garnish with lemon wedges.

SEA BASS MEDITERRANEAN

Serves 2

2 (8-ounce) sea bass fillets

Kosher salt and fresh ground pepper

Flour to dredge

3 tablespoons olive oil

1 cup Marinara Sauce (see page 52)

1 tablespoon Pesto (see page 57)

1 teaspoon capers, rinsed

6 Kalamata olives, pits removed

Pinch crushed red pepper

Preheat oven to 400 degrees. Season fillets with salt and pepper. Dredge fillets in flour, shake off excess. Heat oil in a sauté pan over medium-high heat. Sauté fillets until golden brown on all sides, about 4 minutes. Transfer pan to oven; cook another 5 to 6 minutes. In a separate skillet over medium heat, combine Marinara Sauce, Pesto, capers, olives and crushed red pepper. Remove fillets and place onto a serving platter. Top each fillet with the sauce, making sure olives and capers are resting on top of fish.

FILLET OF SOLE PICATTA

Serves 2

2 (6 to 8-ounce) sole fillets
Flour to dredge
2 eggs, beaten
6 tablespoons unsalted butter, divided
Juice of 1 lemon
1 tablespoon capers, rinsed
Fresh chopped parsley for garnish
Lemon wedges for garnish

Dredge fillets in flour and shake off excess. Dip fillets in egg until well coated. Melt 4 tablespoons butter in a skillet over medium-high heat. Sauté fillets on both sides until golden brown, about 2 to 3 minutes on each side. In a separate skillet over medium heat, combine 2 tablespoons butter, lemon juice, and capers. Heat until butter is melted. When fish is finished, lay fillets on serving platter and top with the butter mixture. Garnish plate with chopped parsley and lemon wedges.

PROSCIUTTO WRAPPED TUNA STEAKS WITH ROSEMARY BUTTER

Serves 4

4 (8-ounce) tuna steaks

Kosher salt and fresh ground pepper to taste

12 slices prosciutto

3 tablespoons olive oil

4 tablespoons butter

2 tablespoons of fresh rosemary leaves

Season steaks with salt and pepper. Wrap each steak with prosciutto, using as many as 3 slices in order to cover steaks completely. Heat olive oil in a large sauté skillet over medium-high heat. Sauté steaks for 2 to 3 minutes on each side for rare and 3 to 4 minutes for medium rare; prosciutto should become crisp. In a small skillet over medium heat, add butter and rosemary leaves and cook until butter is melted. Place steaks on serving platter and top each with the rosemary butter.

BACON WRAPPED MAHI-MAHI
WITH SAUTÉED SPINACH AND MUSHROOMS

Serves 4

4 (6-ounce) mahi-mahi fillets

Cajun seasoning

16 slices thick-sliced bacon

1 pound button mushrooms, sliced

½ cup sliced black olives

½ cup roasted red peppers, julienne

½ cup dry white wine

½ cup Chicken Broth (see page 35)

2 pounds baby spinach, cleaned and dried

Kosher salt and fresh ground pepper

Preheat oven to 450 degrees. Season mahi-mahi with Cajun seasoning. Wrap each fillet with 4 slices of bacon. Place all fillets in an oven-safe baking dish. Bake for 16 minutes, flipping half way. Remove fish from dish and transfer bacon drippings to sauté skillet over medium heat. Add mushrooms, olives and roasted peppers and sauté for 2 to 3 minutes. Add wine and Chicken Broth then reduce by half. After reducing, add spinach and season with salt and pepper. When spinach has wilted, remove from heat. Transfer spinach and mushroom mixture to serving plate, set mahi-mahi on top and drizzle sauce from skillet over the top.

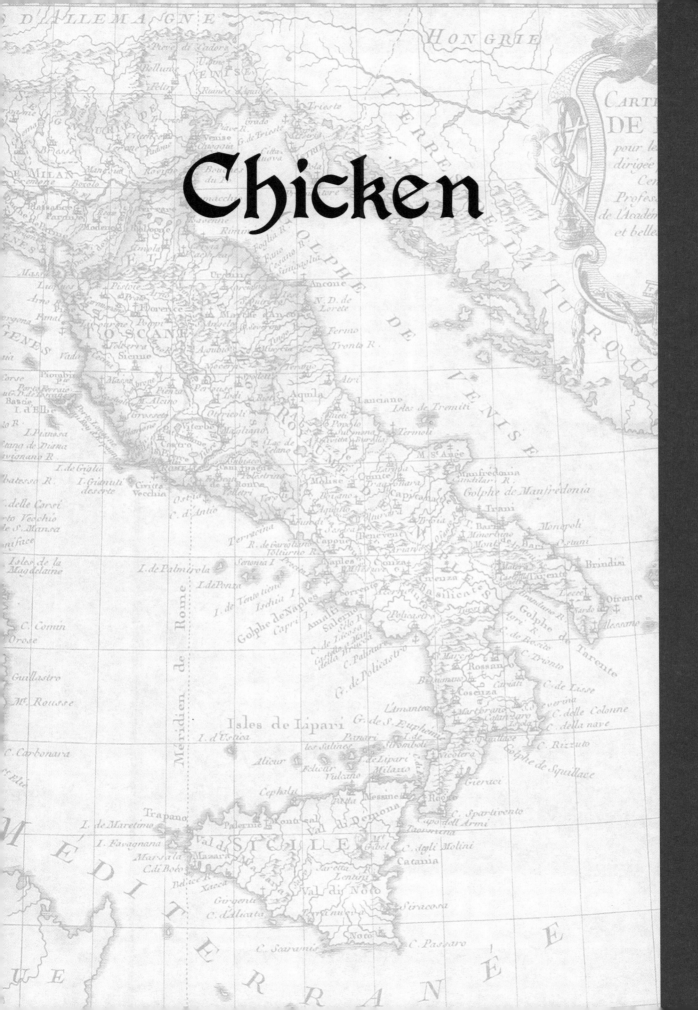

Chicken

Frank, Jr. and family at
Grayton Beach, Florida.

Matchbook from
Grisanti's
on Central.

Larkin and wife Kimberly with
famous Italian chef and Food
Network star Mario Batali.

Grisanti's on Central
(Ashlar Hall)

CHICKEN PARMIGIANA

Serves 4

½ cup grated Parmesan cheese

1 cup seasoned breadcrumbs

4 boneless skinless chicken breasts, lightly pounded to about ½ inch thick

Kosher salt and fresh ground pepper

Flour to dredge

3 eggs, beaten

¼ cup butter

2 tablespoons extra virgin olive oil

1½ cups Marinara Sauce (see page 52)

8 slices mozzarella cheese

Preheat oven to 425 degrees. In a shallow bowl, combine Parmesan cheese and breadcrumbs. Season chicken with salt and pepper. Dredge in flour and shake off excess. Dip chicken in egg until well coated, then dredge in breadcrumb mixture. In a sauté pan over medium-high heat, melt butter with olive oil and sauté chicken for 2 minutes per side or until golden brown. In the bottom of a baking dish, ladle half the Marinara Sauce. Place chicken in dish and spoon remaining Marinara over it. Place 2 slices of cheese on each chicken breast. Bake on center rack of oven for 5 to 6 minutes until bubbling and mozzarella is golden. (Be sure internal temperature of chicken is at least 160 degrees.)

CHICKEN CARCIOFI

Serves 2

2 boneless skinless chicken breasts, lightly pounded to about ½ inch thick
Flour to dredge
3 tablespoons unsalted butter
Zest of ½ lemon
3 medium mushrooms, sliced
¼ cup dry white wine
¾ cup Chicken Broth (see page 35)
4 artichoke hearts, halved
Fresh chopped parsley for garnish

Dredge chicken in flour and shake off excess. In a sauté pan over medium-high heat, melt butter. Sauté chicken in butter 2 to 3 minutes per side until light brown. Add lemon zest, mushrooms, wine and Chicken Broth to the pan. Reduce heat to medium and cook 6 to 7 minutes more until sauce becomes creamy and will coat the back of a metal spoon. If sauce becomes too thick before the 6 minutes are up, add additional ¼ cup Chicken Broth to the pan. Add artichoke hearts and continue to simmer 1 minute more. Transfer chicken to a serving platter, spoon sauce and artichokes over the top and garnish with parsley. (Be sure the internal temperature of chicken is at least 160 degrees.)

WHOLE ROASTED FREE-RANGE CHICKEN

Serves 4

1 (3-pound) whole chicken
Kosher salt and fresh ground pepper
2 tablespoons extra virgin olive oil
2 teaspoons chopped rosemary leaves
2 teaspoons chopped thyme

Preheat oven to 375 degrees. Rinse chicken with cold water and pat dry. Season with kosher salt and fresh ground pepper. Combine olive oil, rosemary and thyme; brush chicken with olive oil blend. Place chicken in a roasting pan and set in oven. Cook for 40 to 45 minutes, making sure to baste the chicken with the herb olive oil mixture 2 to 3 times. The internal temperature should be at least 160 degrees. Allow chicken to rest for 10 minutes before carving.

CHICKEN FOG CITY

Serves 4

*You will need to ask a butcher for the
double lobe chicken breasts that make this dish work so well.*

4 double lobe boneless skinless chicken breasts
½ cup crumbled Gorgonzola cheese
4 artichoke hearts, halved
4 eggs, beaten
Seasoned breadcrumbs to dredge
½ cup butter
1 cup Demi-Glace Sauce (see page 58)

Preheat oven to 425 degrees. Lay the chicken breasts on a cutting board and cover with wax paper. Lightly pound each breast. On one side of the breast, place one fourth of crumbled Gorgonzola cheese and 1 halved artichoke heart. Fold the remaining breast over the stuffed side. Repeat process for each chicken then dip each breast in egg and dredge in seasoned breadcrumbs. Melt butter in a large sauté pan over medium-high heat. Sauté each breast for 3 to 4 minutes per side, until golden brown. Place all breasts in oven to finish cooking. Internal temperature should be at least 160 degrees. To plate the dish, ladle ¼ cup Demi-Glace on each plate and lay stuffed breast on top.

CHICKEN MARSALA

Serves 2

2 boneless skinless chicken breasts, lightly pounded
Flour to dredge
2 tablespoons plus 2 teaspoons unsalted butter, divided
4 medium mushrooms, sliced
¼ cup dry Marsala wine
¾ cup Chicken Broth (see page 35)

Dredge chicken in flour and shake off excess. In a sauté pan over medium-high heat, melt 2 tablespoons butter. Sauté chicken in butter 2 to 3 minutes per side until light brown. Add mushrooms, wine and Chicken Broth to the pan. Reduce heat to medium and cook 6 to 7 minutes more until sauce becomes creamy and will coat the back of a metal spoon. Remove from heat, stir in remaining butter until well-incorporated into sauce and serve. (Be sure the internal temperature of the chicken is at least 160 degrees.)

CHICKEN CACCIATORE

Serves 4

In Italian, cacciatore means "hunter."
This dish can be served alone or with pasta or white rice.

3 tablespoons olive oil

2 garlic cloves

1 medium white onion, sliced

1 large green pepper, cut into 1-inch strips

1 (2½ to 3-pound) fryer chicken, cut up

2 cups peeled, crushed tomatoes

1 cup Marinara Sauce (see page 52)

1 teaspoon dry oregano

1 teaspoon dry rosemary

¼ cup dry white wine

In a heavy bottom pot over medium-high heat, add oil, garlic, onion and pepper. Sauté until onion and pepper become soft, 3 to 4 minutes. Remove garlic cloves and discard. Remove onion and pepper and set aside. Brown chicken pieces on both sides. Add crushed tomatoes, Marinara Sauce and onion and pepper back into the pot. Reduce heat to medium-low and allow chicken to simmer for 20 minutes. Add seasonings and wine to the pot, cover and cook for another 25 minutes until chicken is tender. To serve, remove chicken to serving platter and ladle sauce over the top.

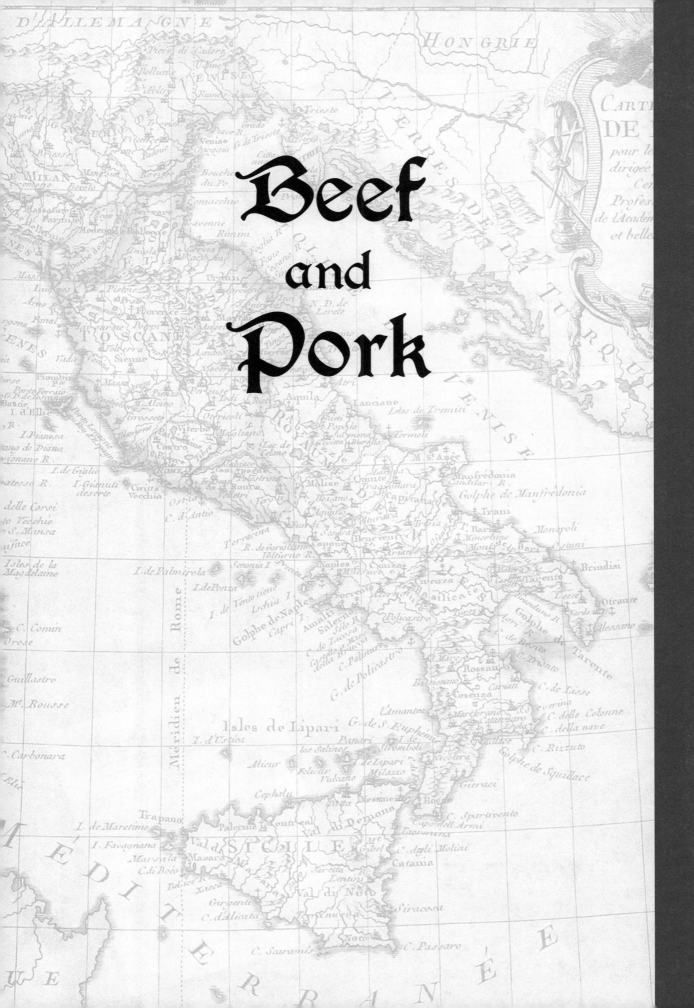

Beef and Pork

THE BLUES BALL

MEMPHIS CHARITABLE FOUNDATION

June 15, 2001

Mr. John Cook
Frank Grisanti
1022 S. Shady Grove
Memphis TN 38120

Dear John,

Thank you for all you did to help make our Blues Ball Bodacious Golf Blast and the "You Ain't Nothin' but a Hound Dog" Clay Shoot a smashing success!

Everyone seemed to have such fun!! That is what happens when you mix great teams, great people, great weather, great causes, great golf, great guns, great margaritas, great Mexicano, great BBQ, great gospel, great motorcycles, Hummers and Flying Boats. . .at a Grand place.

A "phantasmagoric" blend of the best. . .thank you!

Your willingness to donate a door prize when Susan Hedgepeth called is greatly appreciated. Next year we will be challenged to top this one. . .and it will be possible if you will again participate.

Until then, circle your calendars for The Blues Ball, September 22, 2001, (place TBA) and plan to party hardy!

My best,

Pat Kerr Tigrett

PKT/srr

200 WAGNER PLACE · MEMPHIS, TENNESSEE · 38103 · TEL: 901/527-5683 · FAX: 901/526-3578

Frank, Jr. talks with Jackie Aaron, president of Athens Distributing.

Larkin says "I'm not drinking any of this!"

Frank Grisanti

CHEF'S SUMMER FEATURES

INSALATA FRUTTI DI MARE with Tortellini $9.95

OYSTERS NEPTUNE AL FORNO with Bernaise $10.95

LUMACHE FLORENTINE en Cassarole $11.95

POLLO FRA DIABLO with Red Pepper Pasta $11.95

JULIENNE OF SALMON with Dill Linguine $14.95

CHICKEN SALTIMBOCCA with Pasta Alfredo $14.95

LOBSTER GEORGIO with Capelli D Angela $15.95

ENTREE INCLUDES $19.95

MIX GARDEN SALAD AND RASPBERRY SORBET

THE PERFECT NEW YORK STRIP

Serves 4

*This is my favorite dish. If you are having good friends over for dinner,
they will be blown away by these steaks! The key is to have a hot grill and let them cook.
No peeking! I always recommend using charcoal for steaks but gas grilling is fine, too.*

4 (16-ounce) strips

Kosher salt and fresh ground pepper

4 garlic cloves, chopped

4 rosemary sprigs

2 tablespoons extra virgin olive oil

Lay steaks out on a platter. Coat each side of meat with salt and pepper. Spread garlic on each strip. Lay a sprig of rosemary on the top of each steak and drizzle with olive oil. Transfer steaks to refrigerator for 30 to 45 minutes before cooking. Heat grill according to manufacturer's directions and grill steaks for 4 to 5 minutes per side for medium rare turning them only once. For those who prefer their steaks more well done, simply move them off to the sides of the grill so they are not directly over the heat and continue cooking to desired doneness. Allow the strips to rest for at least 10 minutes before serving.

TOURNEDOS GRISANTI

Serves 2

2 (8-ounce) beef fillets, cut in half lengthwise

Kosher salt and fresh ground pepper

Flour to dredge

2 tablespoons unsalted butter

½ cup butter

Splash of dry white wine

1 cup lump crabmeat, picked of all shell pieces

Fresh chopped parsley

½ cup béarnaise sauce

Season fillet halves with salt and pepper. Dredge in flour and shake off excess. In a sauté pan over medium-high heat, melt butter and sauté beef for 4 to 5 minutes per side for medium rare. In a separate skillet over medium heat, melt butter and add wine, crabmeat and parsley. Sauté 3 to 4 minutes. Transfer beef to serving platter, top each with crab mixture and finish by spooning béarnaise sauce over the top.

ITALIAN STYLE PRIME RIB

Serves 6 to 8

We do this dish at the restaurant every Saturday night.
The leftovers are great for cold sandwiches the next day.

1 (3-bone) rib roast, 4 to 6 pounds
½ cup kosher salt
½ cup coarse black pepper
½ cup chopped garlic
½ cup fresh rosemary leaves
1 cup olive oil

Preheat oven to 350 degrees. In a large roasting pan, place roast rib side down. Combine kosher salt, coarse pepper, garlic, rosemary and olive oil in a separate bowl; mix together well. Rub mixture over entire roast. When finished, place roast in oven and allow to cook for 1½ hours. For a medium-rare roast, internal temperature should be 125 degrees (check this with an instant read thermometer inserted into the center). When desired temperature is reached, remove roast and allow to rest for 15 minutes before carving. The internal temperature will rise 5 to 10 degrees while resting.

FRANK'S STEAK SANDWICH

Serves 4

One of our most requested and asked about menu items.
This is the quintessential steak sandwich. The reason why — only a New York Strip will do.
Have the butcher cut strips at just about one pound each.

4 (14-ounce) New York strips, fat removed
Extra virgin olive oil
Kosher salt and fresh ground pepper
4 hoagie buns
2 tablespoons butter, melted

Heat grill according to manufacturer's directions. Lay the strips on a platter and coat each with extra virgin olive oil. Season each strip on both sides with kosher salt and fresh ground pepper. Place strips onto grill and cook for 4 to 5 minutes on the first side; do not move them around during this time. Flip steaks and cook for an additional 3 to 4 minutes to produce a medium-rare steak. When steaks are almost done, split hoagie buns, brush with melted butter and place on grill to toast. Remove steaks from grill and place on buns. Cut sandwiches in half and serve with Homemade Potato Chips (see page 115) or your favorite side dish.

TENDERLOIN GRISANTI STYLE

Serves 4 ·

4 (8-ounce) tenderloin beef fillets
Olive oil
Kosher salt and fresh ground pepper
6 medium mushrooms, sliced
¼ cup flour
2 tablespoons butter
¼ cup dry Marsala wine
1 cup Chicken Broth (see page 35)
½ cup Gorgonzola cheese

Lightly brush each fillet with oil and season with salt and pepper on both sides. Heat grill according to manufacturer's directions. Grill fillets 6 to 7 minutes per side for medium rare. While fillets are cooking, dust mushrooms with flour and shake off excess. In a sauté skillet over medium heat, melt butter and add mushrooms. Sauté for about 2 minutes. Remove skillet from heat and add Marsala wine. Place skillet back on the stove and set heat to medium. Add Chicken Broth and simmer for about 2 minutes until sauce reaches a creamy consistency. When steaks are ready, remove from grill and top each with Gorgonzola cheese and pour Marsala mushroom sauce over the top.

POT ROAST IN RED WINE

Serves 10 to 12

This was a dish that Mr. Rinaldo "Willie" Grisanti would make on Sunday evenings.

1 (6-pound) sirloin pot roast
½ teaspoon dried thyme leaves
¼ teaspoon ground black pepper
1 bay leaf, crumbled
2 pounds small new potatoes
½ pound carrots
1 (12-ounce) package frozen green beans
1 package dry onion soup mix
1¾ cups dry red wine, divided
2 tablespoons flour
Fresh chopped parsley for garnish

Preheat oven to 350 degrees. Place roast on a large sheet of foil and rub with thyme, pepper and bay leaves. Add potatoes, carrots and green beans to foil. Combine soup mix and 1 cup of wine and pour over roast and vegetables. Seal sides of foil and place entire packet in a roasting pan. Cook for 3 hours. Remove roast and vegetables from packet and set aside, leaving juice and drippings. Pour drippings into a separate sauté pan over medium heat. Whisk in remaining ¾ cup wine mixed well with flour; simmer until gravy reaches a creamy consistency. Garnish with fresh parsley.

SLICED BEEF TENDERLOIN
WITH GORGONZOLA CREAM

Serves 2

2 (8-ounce) tenderloin beef fillets
Olive oil
Kosher salt and fresh ground pepper
¾ cup heavy cream
½ cup Gorgonzola cheese

Lightly brush beef with olive oil and season with salt and pepper on both sides. Heat grill according to manufacturer's directions. Grill beef 6 to 7 minutes per side for medium rare. In a heavy saucepan over medium heat, combine cream and cheese. Stirring constantly, bring sauce to a rolling boil. Reduce heat to low and simmer until mixture has reached a creamy consistency and coats the back of a spoon. Once beef fillets have cooled slightly, slice diagonally into ½-inch thick slices. Transfer to serving platter, fan slices out and spoon sauce over the top. Serve with Homemade Potato Chips (recipe follows).

HOMEMADE POTATO CHIPS

2 baking potatoes
Vegetable oil for frying
Kosher salt

Wash potatoes and dry well on paper towels. With a mandoline or other slicing instrument, slice potatoes lengthwise very thin. Heat oil in frying pan over medium-high heat at a depth of 2 to 3 inches. Add potato slices to oil one at a time and fry in small batches until a little darker than golden brown. Transfer to a paper towel lined plate and season immediately with salt. Serve warm.

STEAK PIZZAIOLA

Serves 4

This is a great Italian steak dish that can be done indoors.

4 tablespoons olive oil

2 garlic cloves

½ cup diced onion

Kosher salt and fresh ground pepper

4 (10-ounce) boneless sirloin steaks

2 cups peeled and chopped tomatoes

1 teaspoon oregano

4 fresh basil leaves, chopped

In a large sauté skillet over medium-high heat, add olive oil and garlic cloves. Sauté until garlic turns golden brown. Remove garlic cloves and add onion. Sauté onion until it becomes soft, 3 to 4 minutes. Sprinkle each steak with salt and pepper. Place steaks in the skillet and brown on each side, 2 to 3 minutes per side. Add tomatoes and oregano, lower heat to medium-low and allow steaks to simmer for 10 to12 minutes. To serve, remove steaks to serving platter and top each with the tomato sauce and fresh chopped basil.

PORK CUTLETS
WITH LEMON AND PARMESAN

Serves 4

8 (3-ounce) pork cutlets

1 cup fresh lemon juice

¼ cup grated Parmesan cheese

¼ cup dry white wine

4 tablespoons butter

¼ cup olive oil

Seasoned breadcrumbs

Fresh chopped parsley for garnish

Lemon wedges for garnish

Lay all cutlets on a cutting board and cover with wax paper. Pound cutlets until they are about ⅛-inch thick. In a large bowl combine lemon juice and Parmesan cheese. Add cutlets to lemon juice mixture and let sit for 30 to 45 minutes. In a large sauté skillet over medium heat add wine, butter and olive oil. Dredge cutlets in breadcrumbs and add to the sauté skillet. Cook for 4 to 5 minutes per side, until golden brown. Internal temperature should be at least 150 degrees. Transfer cutlets to serving platter and garnish with fresh chopped parsley and lemon wedges.

ITALIAN STYLE PORK CHOP CASSEROLE

Serves 4

1 tablespoon olive oil
8 (4-ounce) bone-in pork chops
Kosher salt and fresh ground pepper
1 tablespoon chopped garlic
1 large yellow onion, thinly sliced
2 large red potatoes, peeled and thinly sliced
4 sprigs rosemary
1 cup dry white wine

Preheat oven to 350 degrees. Grease an 8x12 casserole dish with olive oil. Season each chop with salt, pepper and chopped garlic. Lay onion in bottom of the casserole, top with potatoes, chops and rosemary sprigs; add wine. Cover and cook for 25 minutes. Be sure internal temperature of pork is at least 150 degrees.

HONEY AND BALSAMIC GLAZED PORK CHOPS

Serves 4

4 (14-ounce) bone-in pork chops
Kosher salt and fresh ground pepper
1 cup honey
½ cup balsamic vinegar

Season each chop with salt and fresh ground pepper. Combine honey and balsamic vinegar; whisk together well and set aside. Using a charcoal grill, allow charcoal to get sufficiently hot. Place chops on the grill and cook for 7 to 8 minutes per side. Internal temperature should be at least 150 degrees. Remove chops to a platter and brush honey balsamic mixture over each and return to grill and cook for additional 1 minute per side. Brush each chop once more before serving.

Veal

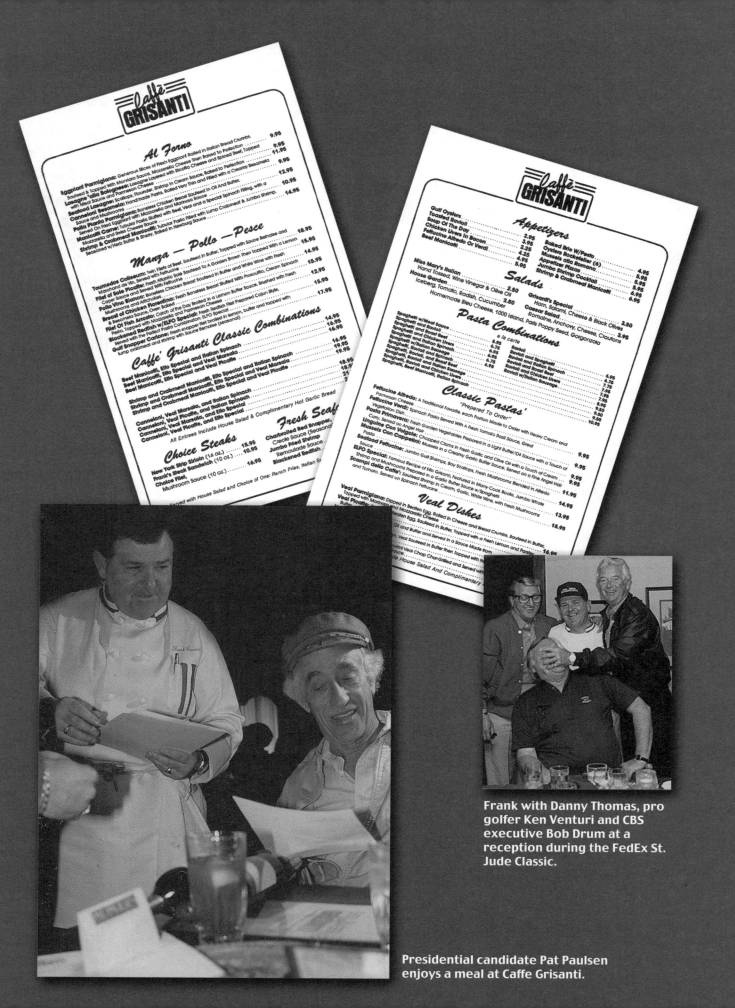

Frank with Danny Thomas, pro golfer Ken Venturi and CBS executive Bob Drum at a reception during the FedEx St. Jude Classic.

Presidential candidate Pat Paulsen enjoys a meal at Caffe Grisanti.

OSSO BUCCO

Serves 4

4 large veal shanks
Kosher salt and fresh ground pepper
3 tablespoons butter
3 tablespoons extra virgin olive oil
Flour
1 large white onion, chopped
½ cup chopped celery
½ cup chopped carrots
½ teaspoon thyme
1 cup dry white wine
2 cups Chicken or Beef Broth (see page 35-36)
2 cups peeled and chopped tomatoes
Gremolada (see recipe below)

Preheat oven to 350 degrees. Season shanks with salt and pepper. Heat butter and olive oil in a Dutch oven over medium-high heat. Dredge shanks in flour and shake off excess. Add shanks to oil in a single layer and brown on all sides. Once browned, remove and set aside. Add onion, celery, carrot and thyme, and sauté 5 minutes. Slowly add wine, using a wooden spoon to scrape any browned bits from the bottom of the pan. Transfer shanks back into pot, and add broth and tomatoes. Liquid should be sufficient to cover shanks. Cover pot and transfer to oven. Cook for 1½ hours, checking occasionally. If liquid level falls below shanks, add just enough broth to keep them covered. To serve shanks, place in serving dish and ladle sauce over the top. Top with Gremolada.

GREMOLADA
1 tablespoon lemon zest
1 tablespoon chopped fresh parsley
1 teaspoon chopped garlic

Combine ingredients.

VEAL CHOP SALTIMBOCCA

4 servings

4 (12 to 14-ounce) veal chops
3 tablespoons extra virgin olive oil
Kosher salt and fresh ground pepper
2 teaspoons rubbed dry sage
4 thin slices prosciutto
4 thin slices provolone cheese
½ cup Demi-Glace Sauce (see page 58)

Heat gas or charcoal grill according to manufacturer's directions. Rub each chop with olive oil, salt and pepper. Place chops on grill and cook for 4 to 5 minutes on each side. Remove chops and top each with sage, prosciutto and provolone cheese. Place back onto grill for 1 to 2 minutes until cheese is melted. Top with equal amounts of warm Demi-Glace.

VEAL FRA DIABLO

Serves 4

1½ pounds sliced veal scallops
Salt and freshly ground pepper
Flour to dredge
3 tablespoons butter
1 cup Marinara Sauce (see page 52)
1 tablespoon Pesto (see page 57)
1 teaspoon capers, rinsed
1 dozen Kalamata olives, pits removed
¼ teaspoon crushed red pepper flakes

Lightly pound veal slices until they are about ¼ inch thick. Sprinkle each veal slice with salt and freshly ground pepper and then dredge in flour. Shake off excess. In a heavy skillet over medium heat, melt butter. Sauté veal until lightly browned on each side. Remove veal slices and set aside. In skillet, add Marinara, Pesto, capers, olives and crushed red pepper. Add veal back to pan and bring to a simmer for about 1 minute. Transfer veal to a serving platter and spoon remaining sauce over the top.

VEAL PARMIGIANA

Serves 4

1½ pounds sliced veal scallops
Kosher salt and freshly ground pepper
Flour to dredge
1½ cups seasoned breadcrumbs for dredging
¼ cup grated Parmesan cheese
2 eggs, beaten
4 tablespoons extra virgin olive oil
1 cup Marinara Sauce (see page52)
4 thin slices mozzarella cheese

Preheat oven to 425 degrees. Lightly pound veal slices until they are about ¼ inch thick. Season each slice with salt and pepper, dredge in flour and shake off the excess. In a shallow bowl, combine breadcrumbs and Parmesan cheese. Dip each slice in egg and then in breadcrumb and Parmesan mixture. Heat olive oil in a heavy skillet over medium heat. Brown meat on both sides and set aside. In an ovenproof baking dish, ladle half the Marinara Sauce on the bottom, add veal slices and spoon remaining Marinara Sauce on top of each. Cover each veal slice with slice of mozzarella cheese. Bake in a 425-degree oven for 8 to 10 minutes.

GRILLED TUSCAN VEAL CHOP

Serves 4

The truffle oil is wonderful on these chops; it adds a great rustic flavor.

4 (12 to 14-ounce) veal chops
3 tablespoons extra virgin olive oil
Kosher salt and fresh ground pepper
1 tablespoon white truffle oil

Heat grill according to manufacturer's directions. Rub each chop with olive oil, salt and pepper. Place chops on the grill, keeping them away from direct flame. Cook each side for 4 to 5 minutes until a meat thermometer inserted in the center reads 145 degrees. When chops are finished, remove from grill and drizzle lightly with truffle oil.

VEAL PICATTA

Serves 4

1½ pounds sliced veal scallops
Salt and freshly ground pepper
Flour to dredge
2 eggs, beaten
4 tablespoons extra virgin olive oil
4 tablespoons butter
1½ tablespoons capers, rinsed
Juice of 2 lemons
Lemon wedges for garnish
Fresh chopped parsley for garnish

Lightly pound veal slices until they are about ¼ inch thick. Season each scallop with salt and pepper. Dredge in flour and shake off excess. Dip each slice into egg, making sure to coat completely. Heat olive oil in a heavy bottom skillet over medium heat. Cook veal on each side until a golden brown crust is formed; about 1 minute per side. Remove veal from pan and lower heat to medium. Discard oil. In skillet, combine butter, capers and lemon juice until butter is melted. Return veal to skillet and turn until well coated with butter mixture. Place on serving platter and garnish with lemon wedges and fresh chopped parsley.

THE PERFECT
NEW YORK
STRIP
Page 109

HONEY AND BALSAMIC GLAZED PORK CHOP

Page 118

MAMA HUNT'S KEY
LIME PIE
Page 135

GRISANTI'S CHOCOLATE CHEESECAKE
Page 131

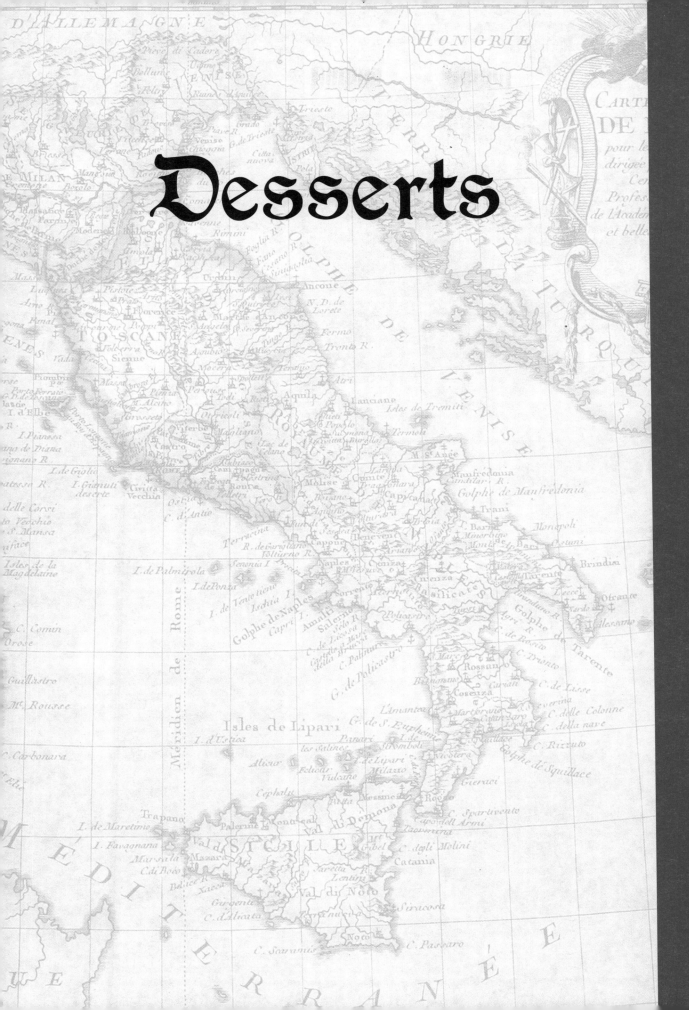

Desserts

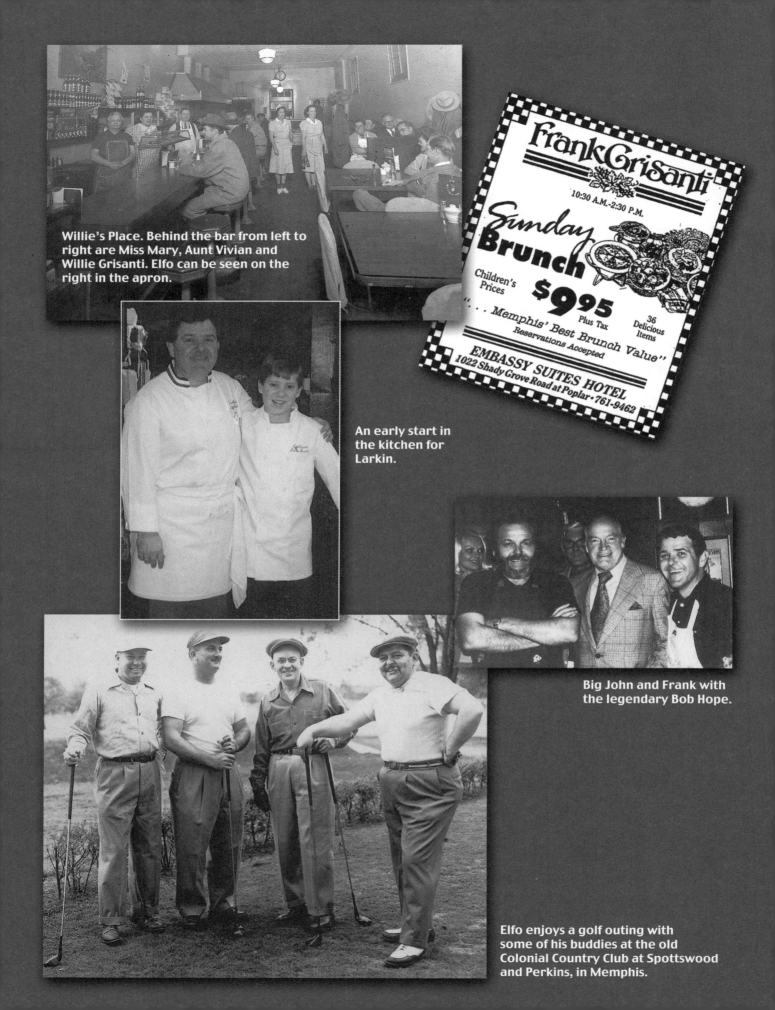

Willie's Place. Behind the bar from left to right are Miss Mary, Aunt Vivian and Willie Grisanti. Elfo can be seen on the right in the apron.

Frank Grisanti

10:30 A.M.-2:30 P.M.

Sunday Brunch $9.95

Children's Prices

Plus Tax

36 Delicious Items

"... Memphis' Best Brunch Value"

Reservations Accepted

EMBASSY SUITES HOTEL
1022 Shady Grove Road at Poplar · 761-9462

An early start in the kitchen for Larkin.

Big John and Frank with the legendary Bob Hope.

Elfo enjoys a golf outing with some of his buddies at the old Colonial Country Club at Spottswood and Perkins, in Memphis.

GRISANTI'S CHOCOLATE CHEESECAKE

About 16 slices

2 pounds cream cheese, at room temperature

1 cup butter

3 cups graham cracker crumbs

1 (12-ounce) package semi-sweet chocolate chips

2 cups sugar

1 tablespoon cocoa

4 eggs

2 teaspoons vanilla

2 cups sour cream

1 cup whipping cream

1 teaspoon sugar

Grated chocolate

Chopped pecans

Maraschino cherries

Remove cream cheese from refrigerator about 2 hours before preparing cheesecake. Melt butter in a medium saucepan over low heat. Add graham cracker crumbs and stir until crumbs are moistened adding additional melted butter in mixture is too crumbly to handle well. Press crumbs into bottom and up the sides of a 10-inch springform pan. Chill. Melt chocolate in top of double boiler over simmering water; remove from heat. Place softened cheese in a large mixing bowl and beat with mixer at medium speed, until cheese is smooth. Beat in sugar gradually, then add cocoa, beating until well combined and smooth. Add eggs, one at a time, beating well after each addition. Add melted chocolate and vanilla, then stir in sour cream and pour into chilled crust. Bake in a 290-degree oven for 1½ hours. Cool at room temperature, then chill at least 5 hours before serving. (Cooked cake will have slight movement in the center, but will become firm as it chills.) Whip cream with 1 teaspoon sugar until very thick. Spoon into a pastry bag and decorate cake. Garnish with grated chocolate or pecans and maraschino cherries. Slice thinly to serve.

SAUTÉED AMARONE APPLES

Serves 6

*I love to make this dish in the fall and use Fuji apples.
Great to spoon over a good vanilla ice cream.*

3 Fuji apples, peeled, cored and cut into ½ inch slices

⅓ cup sugar

6 tablespoons butter, divided

Pinch of cinnamon

1 cup Amarone wine

In a bowl, combine sliced apples and sugar. Lightly toss until apple slices are well coated. Add 4 tablespoons butter to a sauté skillet over medium-high heat. Once butter is melted, add apples and cinnamon. Sauté for 3 to 4 minutes. Add wine to skillet making sure to scrape any bits of food that were stuck to the bottom. Reduce heat to medium-low and cook until sauce becomes creamy. Remove pan from heat and add remaining butter. Stir until butter is well incorporated. Serve immediately.

GRILLED SUMMER PEACHES
WITH BALSAMIC VINEGAR

Serves 6

The key to this recipe and the strawberry dish on the following page is the balsamic vinegar. You want to use good quality vinegar that is at least 10 years old. Remember, you only need to use a small amount to garnish the fruit.

6 ripe peaches, split in half, pits removed

Sugar to sprinkle

Aged balsamic vinegar

Heat grill. Lay peach halves on plate, flesh side up and sprinkle each with sugar. Place peaches on grill flesh side down; cook 3 to 4 minutes until sugar begins to caramelize. To serve, place peaches on a serving platter flesh side up and lightly drizzle the flesh of each with the balsamic vinegar.

STRAWBERRIES
WITH AGED BALSAMIC VINEGAR

Serves 6

This is a quick but wonderful dessert. It is great served over vanilla ice cream.

2 dozen strawberries, stemmed and halved

¼ cup sugar

Aged balsamic vinegar

Vanilla ice cream

Fresh mint leaves for garnish

Place strawberries in a bowl with sugar and toss well. Chill berries for at least 1 hour to macerate (become steeped in liquid). To serve, put a scoop of ice cream in serving dish, top with strawberries and drizzle each dish with a small amount of balsamic vinegar. Garnish each dish with a fresh mint leaf.

ELLEN'S LEMON FLUFF

Serves 8

When serving this dish, I like to garnish the Fluff with fresh blueberries and raspberries.

1 angel food cake

Juice of 4 lemons

1 can sweetened condensed milk

½ cup sugar

1 cup heavy cream

Blackberries or raspberries for garnish

Break angel food cake in bite-size pieces and place in 9x13 casserole dish. In a large bowl, combine lemon juice, condensed milk and sugar. Whisk until well blended. In separate bowl, add heavy cream and whip until small peaks begin to form. Fold whipped cream into lemon mixture. Spoon mixture over angel food pieces. Cover dish with plastic wrap and refrigerate for 1 hour before serving.

SUMMERTIME BLUEBERRY CRUNCH

Serves 8 to 10

2 cups flour
2 sticks butter
1 cup chopped pecans
8 ounces cream cheese (room temperature)
1 (16-ounce) box powdered sugar, sifted
8 ounces Cool Whip, softened
1 can blueberry pie filling

Preheat oven to 350 degrees. In a large bowl combine flour, butter and chopped pecans. Once the ingredients are blended together, press the mixture into the bottom and up the sides of a 13x9 baking dish. Place in oven and cook for 12 to 15 minutes until golden brown.

In another bowl, combine cream cheese, powdered sugar and Cool Whip. Once these are well blended, spoon the mixture into the cooled crust. To finish, spread blueberry filling over the top of dish and chill for 1 hour. When ready, cut into squares and serve.

LEMON AND LIME GRANITA

Serves 4

This is a very refreshing summertime dessert.

1 cup fresh lemon juice
1 cup fresh lime juice
⅓ cup water
Zest of ½ lemon
Zest of ½ lime
⅓ cup sugar
Fresh mint leaves for garnish

Combine all ingredients except mint leaves. Pour mixture into a shallow pan and place in freezer for 1½ to 2 hours. During the freezing process, stir mixture every 20 to 25 minutes. This will help create a slushy consistency. When ready to serve, spoon mixture into chilled glasses and garnish with fresh mint leaves.

MAMA HUNT'S KEY LIME PIE

Serves 8

Don't hesitate to use a commercially prepared pie crust.
They are delicious and can save about 15 minutes of prep time!

1 (9-inch) graham cracker crust

FILLING:
1 can sweetened condensed milk
3 egg yolks
Zest of 1 lime
¾ cup fresh squeezed lime juice

TOPPING:
2 cups heavy whipping cream
2 tablespoons sugar
Zest of ½ lime for garnish

Preheat oven to 375 degrees. In a large mixing bowl, add egg yolks and whisk for 2 to 3 minutes. Add condensed milk into the eggs and whisk until well combined. To finish the filling, add lime juice and zest, mix together well for 2 to 3 minutes. Pour mixture into pie crust. Set pie plate in a 10x13 baking pan; create a water bath by adding a small amount of water in bottom of pan. The water level should reach ½ inch below the top of the pie crust. Bake for 8 to 10 minutes, until filling has set. Test by sliding a toothpick into the middle of the pie. If it comes out clean, it has set. Allow the pie to cool and refrigerate until ready to serve.

For topping, add heavy cream into a large bowl. Whip with a wire whisk for 3 to 4 minutes. Add sugar and continue to whisk until small peaks begin to form. When ready to serve, remove pie and place whipped cream on top. Using a rubber spatula, spread whipped cream evenly over the entire pie. Top with the remaining lime zest for garnish and cut into 8 pieces.

APRICOT SQUARES

Makes 9 (3-inch) squares

This is a great dessert to keep in the house around the holidays.
It's sure to become a family favorite.

CRUST:
1¼ cups flour
⅓ cup brown sugar
½ cup butter, melted
¾ cup apricot preserves

Preheat oven to 350 degrees. Mix first 3 ingredients and pat into the bottom of a greased 9-inch square pan. Bake 15 to 20 minutes until just golden brown. Remove from oven.

Spread crust with apricot preserves to within 1 inch of the sides.

TOPPING:
¾ cup flour
½ cup brown sugar
¼ cup butter, softened
⅛ teaspoon salt
½ teaspoon almond extract

Stir ingredients together with a fork until it forms a crumb-like mixture. Cover apricot preserves and bake another 20 to 25 minutes until golden brown.

ICING:
¾ cup powdered sugar
1 tablespoon milk

Combine well. Drizzle over dessert. Cool and cut into 3 inch squares to serve.

TIRAMISU

Serves 4

4 eggs, separated
4 tablespoons sugar
16 ounces mascarpone cheese
1½ cups espresso
½ cup Kahlúa
2 dozen ladyfingers
Cocoa powder to sprinkle

Whip egg whites until peaks form. In a separate bowl, whip yolks and sugar until well combined. Add mascarpone to egg yolk and sugar mixture. Fold egg whites into mascarpone mixture. In another bowl, combine espresso and Kahlúa. Dip half the ladyfingers in coffee mixture and line the bottom of an 8x8 baking dish; spread with part of mascarpone mixture. Repeat process with remaining ladyfingers and mascarpone. Sprinkle top with cocoa powder. Refrigerate for at least 1 hour before serving.

CHRISTMAS COOKIES

Makes 2 to 3 dozen

These cookies have always been a staple in our family during Christmas holidays.

½ pound butter, at room temperature
1½ cups powdered sugar, sifted and divided
2 cups cake flour, sifted
¾ cup chopped pecans
1 teaspoon vanilla

Preheat oven to 350 degrees. With an electric mixer, cream butter and ½ cup powdered sugar. Add flour, pecans and vanilla and mix until well combined. Remove dough and form cookies into crescent shapes on baking sheet. Bake for 12 to 15 minutes until golden brown. While cookies are still warm, dust them heavily with remaining powdered sugar.

CHERRY SPUMONI

An easy "at-home" version of a traditional Italian frozen dessert.

1½ cups heavy cream

½ cup sweetened condensed milk

½ teaspoon rum flavoring

1 (21-ounce) can cherry pie filling

1 cup pitted fresh sweet cherries

⅓ cup miniature chocolate chips

⅓ cup slivered almonds, toasted

Combine heavy cream, sweetened condensed milk and rum flavoring in a large bowl; mix well. Refrigerate 30 minutes.

Lightly grease inside of a 9x5x3 loaf pan. Cut a piece of plastic wrap 24-inches long. Line bottom and sides of pan with plastic wrap so that several inches of wrap overhang each long side.

Remove cream mixture from refrigerator. Beat with electric mixer on high speed 3 to 4 minutes or until soft peak form. Do not overbeat. Fold in cherry pie filling, fresh sweet cherries, chocolate chips and almonds. Spoon mixture evenly into lined pan. Cover and freeze at least 5 hours or overnight.

To serve, quickly dip pan in hot water, immersing just the bottom and halfway up the sides to help release ice cream. Using overhanging plastic wrap for handles, gently lift spumoni from pan and transfer to serving plate. Remove plastic wrap by lifting spumoni with metal spatula. Cut crosswise into slices and serve immediately.

Kitchen Essentials and Glossary

Kitchen Essentials and Glossary

KITCHEN ESSENTIALS FOR ITALIAN COOKING

SPICES:

Italian seasoning	Ground black pepper
Crushed red pepper	Cayenne pepper
Kosher salt	Ground thyme
Garlic powder	Ground oregano
Bay leaf	

PANTRY:

Extra virgin olive oil	Arborio rice
Red wine vinegar	Polenta
Garlic cloves	Tomato paste
Balsamic vinegar	Whole peeled tomatoes
Penne pasta	Pine nuts
Spaghetti pasta	Flour

REFRIGERATOR:

Butter	Kalamata olives
Dijon mustard	Roasted red peppers
Eggs	Anchovy fillets
Capers	Crumbled Gorgonzola cheese
Sun-dried tomatoes	Artichoke hearts
Fresh lemons	Fresh basil
Parmesan block	Pepperoncini peppers
Fresh mozzarella	

GLOSSARY OF ITALIAN
AND OTHER CULINARY TERMS

AGNOLOTTI: Disk or square-shaped pieces of pasta filled and folded with meat and vegetables. They are either served in a broth or with a sauce.

AL DENTE: Pasta cooked al dente should have a somewhat chewy texture and should not break or become mushy when mixed with desired condiments.

AMARETTO: A cookie made of almonds, sugar and egg white, crunchy on the outside and soft and chewy on the inside. Also, a liqueur that tastes like almonds.

ANISE: An herb that tastes like licorice. It is often used in pastries, cheeses, etc.

ANTIPASTO: An appetizer or hors d'oeuvre. Antipasto literally means "before the meal".

ARAGOSTA: Spiny lobster

BACCALA: Cod preserved in salt.

BAGNA CAUDA: (hot bath). A sauce dip made of oil, garlic and anchovies.

BALSAMIC VINEGAR: Balsamic vinegar is a very fine aged vinegar made in Modena, Italy. It is expensive but is the favorite vinegar of most chefs because of its sweet, mellow flavor.

BASIL: An aromatic herb widely used in Mediterranean cooking. It is used in pesto sauce, salads and cooking fish.

BATTUTO: Finely chopped herbs, such as parsley, garlic added raw to a finished dish. When cooked, it is called soffritto.

BASMATI RICE: A long-grain rice with a nutty flavor.

BAY: Dried bay leaves are used frequently in poultry, fish and meat dishes as well as stocks and soups.

BÉARNAISE: One of the classic French sauces. It is made with emulsified egg yolks, butter, fresh herbs, and shallots. It is often served with poultry, grilled fish, and meat.

BÉCHAMEL: It is also one of the basic French sauces. It is a sauce made from white roux, milk or cream, onions and seasonings.

BEURRE BLANC: It is a white butter sauce made from shallots, white wine vinegar and white wine that has been reduced and thickened with heavy cream and unsalted butter. Salt and white pepper to taste.

BEURRE MANIE: A paste of flour and butter used to thicken sauces.

BIANCO (IN): A term which generally indicates a boiled dish without, or with very little condiment.

BISQUE: A thick seafood soup usually made from oysters, shrimp or lobster and thickened with cream.

BISTECCA ALLA FLORENTINA: A thick slice of young beef cut from the rib with the filet still attached. Similar to a T-bone steak; it should be at least 1 inch thick and large enough for 2 to 3 people. It is grilled, usually without greasing it.

BLANCH: The purpose is to loosen the skin on a fruit or vegetable by placing it in hot water for a few minutes and then into cold water to stop the cooking process.

BRAISE: The slow cooking of food in a tight container with a flavoring liquid equal to about half the amount of the main ingredient.

BRIE: A soft cows' milk cheese made in the French region of Brie.

BRÛLÉ: A French word for "burnt" and refers to a caramelized coating of sugar, such as a topping for crème brûlée.

BRUSCHETTA: Slices of a large crusty loaf of toasted bread, rubbed with garlic cloves and seasoned with extra virgin olive oil, salt and pepper to taste. Chopped tomatoes may be added.

BUCATINI: Thick spaghetti with a hole through the middle.

CALZONE: One of the most famous Neapolitan specialties, calzone is a disk of pizza dough filled with prosciutto, mozzarella, ricotta, and parmigiano cheese, folded over in a crescent shape.

CANNELLINI: Small, white beans, slightly elongated and arched in form. They are very common in Tuscany, where they are prepared al fiasco.

CANNELLONI: Cylindrical rolls of fresh egg pasta, which are boiled, then filled. They are stuffed with meat, vegetables, and/or cheese, then baked.

CAPELLI D' ANGELO: (Angel's hair). Very thin spaghetti, usually cooked in broth. Fried and sweetened with honey, they are a Sicilian dessert.

CAPER: The pickled bud of a flowering caper plant. It is found on the Mediterranean coast. Capers are often used as a condiment in salads, used in making tartar sauce and as a seasoning in broiling fish.

CAPON: A castrated male chicken

CAPONATA: A combination of cooked vegetables, capers, olives, and anchovies drizzled with oil and vinegar.

CAPPELLETTI: (little hats). Fresh egg dough pasta filled with meat or a combination of cheese, eggs, and spices. They are rather small and shaped like an Alpine hat.

CAPRINO: Fresh goat's or cow's cheese have a cylindrical shape.

CARBONARA (ALLA): Spaghetti sauce made of browned pancetta, raw egg yolks mixed with parmigiano cheese, and cream.

CARDAMOM: A member of the ginger family. It has a spicy flavor and is used in Indian and Middle Eastern dishes.

CARPACCIO: Very thin sliced raw beef seasoned with oil, lemon, salt, and pepper or other sauces. The dish was served for the first time at Harry's Bar in Venice and named after a Venetian painter.

CAYENNE PEPPER: Red chili pepper that is dried and ground fine for home use.

CHERVIL: An herb belonging to the parsley family. It is best used fresh because of its delicate flavor.

CHIFFONADE: Leafy vegetables such as spinach and lettuce cut into thin strips.

CHIPOTLE: A brownish-red chili pepper that has been dried and smoked and sometimes canned. This chili pepper has a smoky flavor and is very hot.

CHIVE: A member of the onion family used in flavoring foods.

CHUTNEY: A sweet and/or sour seasoning that can be made from fruits and vegetables and flavored with many kinds of spices.

CILANTRO: A fresh coriander leaf.

CLARIFIED BUTTER: Butter that has been heated to remove the impurities.

CONDIMENT: Any seasoning, spice, sauce, relish, etc. used to enhance food at the table.

CONSOMMÉ: A clear strained stock, usually clarified, made from poultry, fish, meat or game and flavored with vegetables.

COPPA: Sausage made from deboned pork neck that is salted and marinated in wine. It is aged, but not allowed to harden.

CORIANDER: A member of the carrot family. Fresh coriander is also called cilantro. This herb is prized for its dried seeds and fresh leaves and is used in similar ways to parsley.

COSTOLETTA: A boneless cutlet of veal or pork, usually taken from the leg, pounded flat, breaded and sautéed in butter or a combination of butter and oil. They can also be prepared in involtini.

COULIS: A thick sauce or purée made from cooked vegetables, fruits, etc.

COUSCOUS: Traditional couscous is generally made from coarsely ground semolina, a wheat flour used for pasta. It is popular in the Mediterranean areas of Morocco and Algeria. If is often served over vegetables or meats along with sauces.

COZZE: Mussels

CRESPELLE: Thin pancakes made with flour, milk, and egg. Prepared like crêpes.

CROSTINO/CROSTONE: Crustless slice of bread cut in different shapes - depending on what it is intended for - either fried in oil or in butter, or toasted in the oven.

CUMIN: A spice from the seeds of the cumin plants. It is often used in making pickles, chutneys and especially in curries.

DEGLACER: A process of dissolving cooking juices left in a pan where meats or poultry have been cooked. This is achieved by adding liquids such as stock or wines to the sediment and then reducing it to half the volume. The sauce is then strained and seasoned.

DEMI-GLACE: A brown sauce boiled and reduced by half.

DIJON MUSTARD: Mustard made from a white wine base.

FAGIOLI: Beans

FARFALLE: "Butterfly"-shaped pasta

FETA CHEESE: A soft and crumbly goat's milk cheese often used in salads.

FETTUCCINE: Fresh ribbon-like pasta

FILO (phyllo): A very thin dough that contains little fat and is used for strudel, baklava and other pastries.

FINOCCHIO: (fennel). A celery-like vegetable with a delicate anise flavor. May be eaten raw or cooked in various ways, such as braised, fried, and boiled.

FLAN: An open custard tart made in a mold. Caramel cream custard is a popular flan dessert.

FOCACCIA: Cake or savory pie

FOIE GRAS: The enlarged liver of a fattened or force-fed goose.

FONDUTA: A fluid and creamy cheese melt made by slowly melting fontina cheese in milk, then mixing in egg yolks.

FONTINA: A rich, mellow, flavorful cheese from Val d'Aosta. It is a delicious melting or eating cheese.

FORMAGGIO: Cheese. There are various types.

FRITTATA: A flat omelet. It may contain vegetables, meat, or cheese. (Particularly parmigiano). Frittate are often served at room temperature.

FRITTO (UL): An assortment of fried foods which may include vegetables, meats, and fish.

FRUTTI DI MARE: Seafood. The term refers to all types of shellfish only, e.g. insalta di frutti di mare (seafood salad).

FUNGHI: Mushrooms, various types

FUSILLI: Spaghetti or short pasta twisted into a long spiral. Short twisted pasta can also be called eliche (propellers).

GAMBERO: Shrimp. A crustacean without claws, it can reach a length of 10 inches; its shell can range from pink to bright red, the meat a delicate pink.

GNOCCHI: Small dumplings made of cooked potatoes, egg, and flour.

GORGONZOLA: A strong Italian blue cheese.

GRANITA: Light slush-ice made with sugar syrup and either fruit juice or coffee.

GREMOLATA: A battuto made of garlic, rosemary, parsley, and lemon peel, used on osso buco.

GRISSINO: Breadsticks made of dough with butter and another fat added. The most traditional ones are those from Torino which are pulled by hand and are very long and irregular in shape.

INFUSE: To soak spices, herbs, or vegetables in a liquid to extract their flavor.

JULIENNE: Vegetables and meats cut into thin strips.

KALAMATA: Kalamata are large black Greek olives.

KALE: A frilly, leafy vegetable of the cabbage family.

LASAGNE: Fresh pasta cut into wide strips.

LEEK: A member of the onion family. Leeks are used in soups, casseroles, etc.

LINGUINE: Long, flat, dried pasta about ⅛ inch wide.

MACCHERONI: Dried, short, tubular pasta, smooth or ribbed.

MARINARA: A tomato sauce flavored with herbs and garlic, usually served with pasta.

MARZAPANE: Almond dough.

MASCARPONE: A rich, dense, fresh triple-cream cheese made from cow's milk. Very fresh mascarpone (seldom seen in the U.S.) is vaguely sweet. It is used both in desserts and savory dishes.

MERLOT: A red-wine grape that produces a fruity flavor.

MESCLUN: A mixture of cut vegetables: usually carrot, onion, celery and sometimes ham or bacon - used to flavor sauces and as a bed on which to braise meat.

MEZZALUNA: (half moon). Crescent-shaped knife with one handle at each end, used for mincing vegetable, meats and other foodstuff.

MINESTRONE: A soup made of various vegetables, rice, or pasta cooked in a broth.

MORTADELLA DI BOLOGNA: Large, cooked salame made of pork and usually mixed with other meats, seasoned with pepper and pistachio nuts. It is easily recognizable by its broad pink slices with chunks of white fat.

MOZZARELLA: A fresh cheese from Southern Italy, mainly from the Campania region. The best quality mozzarella is made with Bufala milk (a breed not to be confused with the American buffalo). In other parts of Italy this same cheese is made with cow's milk generally under the name "fior di latte." The mozzarella has soft and elastic texture, oval-round shape, and white color. Its taste is sweet and milky. It is solid in various shapes: braids, balls, and bite-size pieces.

ORECCHIETTE: Fresh pasta made of only flour and water and shaped into a curl.

OREGANO: Oregano is an herb very similar to marjoram but more pungent. It is widely used in Italian cooking.

OSSO BUCO: Veal shank cut across into thick slices, braised and customarily served with risotto Milanese.

ORZO: Rice-shaped pasta; in Italian the word means barley.

PANCETTA: The salt-cured belly fat of a hog. Pancetta has deep pink stripes of flesh (similar to American bacon) and is used to lard meats and to flavor soups, sauces and other dishes. It may be cured in either a flat or rolled form.

PANE: Breads. Various types.

PAPRIKA: A variety of red bell pepper that has been dried and powdered and made into a cooking spice.

PANNETTONE: Milanese sweet bread made with yeast dough, raisins and candied fruit peelings. It can be done dome-shaped or flat.

PANZANELLA: A salad of stale bread softened in water and vinegar with various vegetables (often coarsely chopped) and dressed with oil and vinegar.

PAPPA AL POMODORO: Tuscan soup made of stale crusty country bread, fresh tomatoes, garlic, basil, pepper, and oil.

PAPPARDELLE: Long, wide strips of fresh pasta.

PARMIGIANA: (alla): A food term which refers to preparation that always contains parmigiano cheese. In Southern Italy the term refers to a dish consisting of fried slices of eggplant layered with tomato sauce, mozzarella cheese and baked.

PARMIGIANO-REGGIANO: a COW'S MILK HARD CHEESE FROM THE REGION AROUND Parma, it is the choicest type of parmigiano. Reggiano is produced under the strictest regulations: it must be made with milk produced between April 1st and November 11th, in the provinces of Parma, Reggio, Modena, Mantua, and Bologna. It is a hand-made cheese aged a minimum of 18 months before it is sold. Authentic Reggiano has the words "Parmigiano-Reggiano" etched in a continuous pattern of small dots around the entire circumference of the rind. It is eaten on its own, used in cooking and for grating.

PARMESAN: A type of parmigiano cheese which can be made all over the world.

PASTA AL FORNO: Baked pasta with ragu and the addition of other ingredients.

PECORINO: A sheep's milk cheese (pecora is Italian for sheep), pecorino can be mild or sharp in flavor, and of hard (for grating) or soft consistency. In the U. S. the most common form of pecorino is romano, a typical Roman cheese. In Italy, two other types of pecorino are: pecorino sardo (from Sardinia), and the pecorino made in Tuscany.

PENNE: Tube-shaped pasta cut on the diagonal.

PEPERONCINO: A thin, long and pointed pepper, either red or green, it varies in intensity from mild to very hot. It may be dried whole or coarsely or finely ground.

PEPPERONI: An Italian salami of pork and beef seasoned with hot red peppers.

PESCE: Fish. Various types.

PESTO: Cold Lingurian sauce made of basil, garlic, parmigiano and pecorino cheeses and oil. It is used on trenette, gnocchi and in minestrone.

PICCATA: Veal scaloppini sautéed very quickly in a pan with butter and lemon juice, Marsala and other ingredients.

PIGNOLI: Pine nuts, also called pinoli.

PIZZAIOLA (alla): A term used to describe stews and sauces made with tomatoes, capers, oregano and anchovies.

POLENTA: Yellow cornmeal, either finely or coarsely ground, cooked with water and seasoned with butter and parmigiano. Polenta may vary in consistency from a soft to a solid form, according to its attended use. In some regions of Italy, white cornmeal or buckwheat flour is used instead of yellow cornmeal.

POLPETTA: (meatball). A mixture of grounded meat, bread, herbs, and cheese formed into balls and fried. Polpette are also cooked in a tomato sauce for pasta. Polpette are often made using leftover bits of meats and vegetables.

POMODORO: Italian for tomato.

PORCINI: Wild mushrooms with large, meaty, brown caps slightly rounded on top. The stems are fleshy and wider at the bottom.

PORTOBELLO: A large cultivated field mushroom that has a firm texture and is ideal for grilling and as a meat substitute.

PROSCIUTTO: (Italian ham) A hog's leg, salted, aged and dressed according to local usage. There are various types of prosciutto.

PROVOLONE: A firm cheese with a pungent, somewhat salty flavor. It can also be mild.

PURÉE: Food that is pounded, finely chopped, or processed through a blender or strained through a sieve to achieve a smooth consistency.

PUTTANESCA (alla): A pasta sauce made of tomato, black olives, anchovies, capers, peperoncino and basil.

RADICCHIO: The red and white leaf chicory of the Veneto region. Radicchio di Treviso or trevigiano refer to the type grown in the Treviso area. It has tender, large leaves with white ribs and red edges. The redicchio of Castelfranco grows in small, tight heads with wide, tightly cupped leaves (similar to iceberg) having white ribs and red edges.

RAVIOLI: Disk or squares of fresh egg pasta stuffed with vegetables, or cheese or meat. The larger ones are generally served with butter, sage and parmigiano cheese. Smaller ones (raviolini) are served with various condiments or in broths.

REDUCE: To boil down a liquid to thicken its consistency and concentrate its flavor.

RICOTTA: A fresh white cheese made with whey. It has the texture and consistency of farmer's or pot cheese and is made in both sweet and savory dishes. Ricotta romana is made with sheep's milk. There is also a salted version which can be aged and used for grating.

RIGATINO: a Tuscan pancetta made with the leanest part of the hog's belly, covered in black pepper and cured flat.

RISOTTO: A preparation of long-grain Italian rice. The basic recipe uses rice, onions, butter, broth and parmigiano. Risotto is cooked slowly, adding small amounts of liquid at a time, and finished by adding butter and parmigiano. Variations may add fish, shellfish, vegetables, sausage, proscuitto, herbs, saffron, and other cheeses besides parmigiano.

ROSEMARY: A shrub with aromatic needle-like leaves. It is used fresh or dried as an herb, especially with lamb, pork and veal.

ROUILLE: A spicy red pepper and garlic mayonnaise.

ROUX: A mixture of flour and fat (usually butter or shortening) cooked together slowly to form a thickening agent for sauces, gumbos, and other soups.

SALAME: Ground meat, seasoned and packed into a casing.

SALSICCIA: Pork meat in casing. It may be consumed fresh, pan-fried or cooked in sauce. It may also be dry-aged.

SALTIMBOCCA: Veal scaloppini rolled with prosciutto and briskly sautéed in butter, sage and white wine.

SCALOPPINA: Thinly sliced lean veal form the center cut of the leg, rib, loin, or square cut chuck, which has been lightly pounded flat. One scaloppina may weigh 1 to 21/2 ounces.

SCAMPO: A prawn measuring up to 10 inches.

SEC: Means dry.

SHALLOT: A sweet member of the onion family. It has a more delicate flavor than regular onions.

SHIITAKE: It is a dark brown mushroom with a meaty flavor. It is available both fresh and dried. It was originally from Japan but is now cultivated in both America and Europe.

SOPPRESSATA: Cooked and aged salame made from the meat taken from the head of the pig, lard spices and pistachio nuts.

SORBETTO: Sherbet, usually made with juice or pulp of fruit.

SORREL: A leafy plant often used in salads, soups, omelets, purées, and sauces. It has a distinct lemon taste.

SPUMONI: Spumoni can also be called semifreddo. All semifreddi or spumoni may be served with an appropriate sauce. These range from a simple fruit sauce to a vanilla cream.

SWEAT: To sauté in a covered vessel until natural juices are exuded.

TAGLIATELLE/TAGLIATELLINE/TAGLIOLINI: Fresh pasta, between .08 of an inch and .02 of an inch wide.

THYME: A herb with a pungent smell that belongs to the same family as mint. It is used in soups, stocks, casseroles and stews.

TIRAMISU: A cold dessert made with layers of sponge cake or lady fingers soaked in coffee and covered with a mascarpone cream.

TORTELLI: Sweet fritters or ravioli stuffed with vegetables, pumpkin, and/or cheese.

TORTELLINI: Stuffed pasta, similar to cappelletti, but shaped into a closed ring.

TOURNEDOS: A trimmed cut of beef or veal fillet.

TRIPPA: (tripe). The stomach and the first part of the intestines of cows, hogs and lamb. This is part of the frattaglie (innards) and is sold already cleaned and par-boiled.

VALDOSTANA: A veal chop sliced open like a pocket and stuffed with fontina, then breaded and fried in butter.

VEAL: The meat of milk-fed baby beef.

VERMICELLI: A thin Italian pasta.

VINAIGRETTE: A basic dressing of oil and vinegar with salt, pepper, herbs, and sometimes mustard.

VITELLO TONNATO: Cold dish of veal with tuna sauce. The lean veal is marinated and cooked in white wine, then sliced and covered with a tuna, anchovy, and caper sauce.

ZABAINOE/ZABAGLIONE: A mixture of egg yolks, Marsala, and sugar beaten in a double boiler until fluffy. It is served warm, in dessert cups or cold with fruit.

ZEST: The outer skin of citrus where the important oils have accumulated.

ZITE/ZITI: Long, cylindrical, hollow dried maccheroni.

ZUPPA: A dense, semi-liquid soup made by cooking meat, fish, shellfish dried beans or vegetables in water. Zuppe are usually served with slices or cubes of toasted or leftover country bread.

ZUPPA INGLESE: An Italian version of English trifle; sponge cake soaked in alchermes and layered with vanilla cream, chocolate, and fruit preserve.

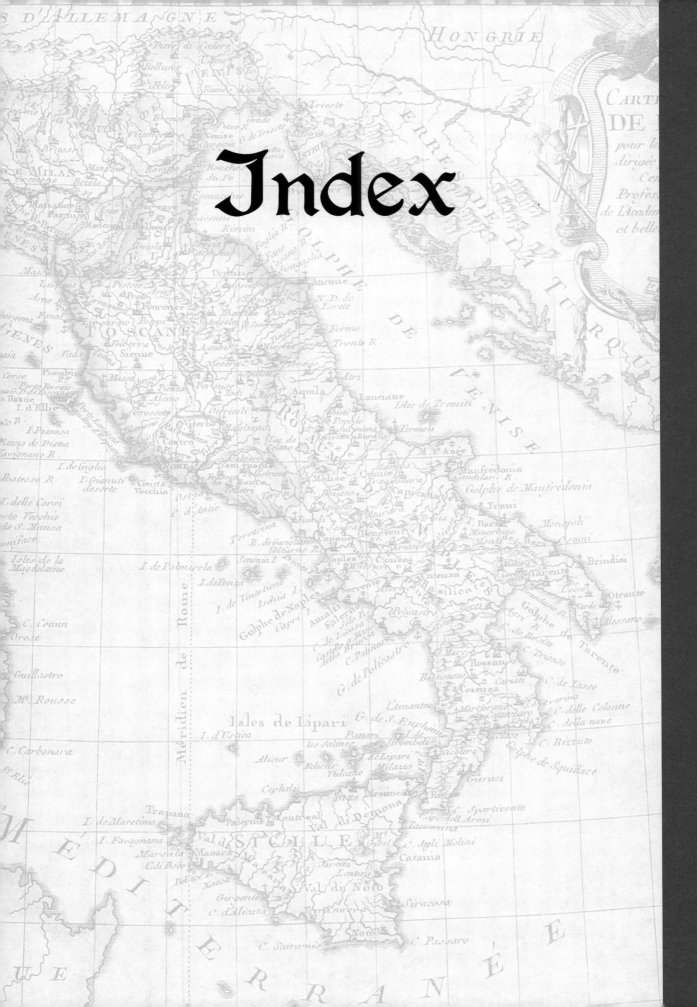

Index

Vincent Price, famous actor and gourmet cook used the Elfo Special and Miss Mary's Salad in his cookbook.

Frank with former Tennessee Governor Don Sundquist.

Frank Grisanti & Sons
The Main Course Cookbook
Wimmer Cookbooks
4650 Shelby Air Drive
Memphis, TN 38118
901-345-8480   800-548-2537
To order online, visit Wimmerco.com

Italian Dining with a 96 Year Tradition

Name: _____

Address: _____

City: _____ State: _____ Zip: _____

Phone: _____ Cell: _____

Please reserve_____ copies of "Collectors Limited Edition"   @ $35.00 each $_____
   (only 4 books per customer)

Please reserve_____ copies of Regular Edition book   @ $25.00 each $_____
   (no limit)

Shipping and Handling   @ $ 5.00 each $_____

Tennessee Residents only add 9.25% each book for sales tax $_____

Total enclosed: $_____

Make checks payable to: Wimmer Cookbooks.

Please charge to: ☐ Visa ☐ MasterCard   Card number _____

Expiration Date: _____   Signature: _____

Mail to Wimmer Cookbooks at above address.

- -

Frank Grisanti & Sons
The Main Course Cookbook
Wimmer Cookbooks
4650 Shelby Air Drive
Memphis, TN 38118
901-345-8480   800-548-2537
To order online, visit Wimmerco.com

Italian Dining with a 96 Year Tradition

Name: _____

Address: _____

City: _____ State: _____ Zip: _____

Phone: _____ Cell: _____

Please reserve_____ copies of "Collectors Limited Edition"   @ $35.00 each $_____
   (only 4 books per customer)

Please reserve_____ copies of Regular Edition book   @ $25.00 each $_____
   (no limit)

Shipping and Handling   @ $ 5.00 each $_____

Tennessee Residents only add 9.25% each book for sales tax $_____

Total enclosed: $_____

Make checks payable to: Wimmer Cookbooks.

Please charge to: ☐ Visa ☐ MasterCard   Card number _____

Expiration Date: _____   Signature: _____

Mail to Wimmer Cookbooks at above address.

GOLPHE DE LYON

GOLPHE DE GENES

DUCHE DE MILAN

Casal · Cremone · Bozolo · Mangoua
Turin · Asti · Tortone · Duché de Parme · Bexel
Albe · Alexandrie · Bobbio · Massa · Parme · Modene
Salue · Aqui · Genes · Brignan
Fossano · Casale · DE GENES
Nice · SEIGNEURIE · Savone
Monaco · Final · Albenga · Massa · Luques · Pisto
C. delle melle · Arno R. · Bma
Oneille · Pl Livourne · TO
I. de Gorgona · Vada · Cecna · S

I. de Capraia

I. de Centuria · C. Corse · Piombin · Plo
G. St Fiorenze · Porto Ferraio · au G. D. de Descen
la Bascie · I. d'Elbe · Porto Longone au Bu de Praun
Calvi · Nebbio · Golo R. · I. Pianosa
I. DE CORSE · Acria · Etang de Diana
Tavignano R.
Capo Rosso · Corte · I. de Giglio
G. de Ginevra · Adjazzo · Albatesso R. · I. Gianuti deserte
G. d'Adjazzo
G. de Talabo · I. delle Corsi
Porto Vecchio
G. de S. Mansa
St Boniface · St Boniface
I. d'Asinaria · Detroit d' · Isles de la Magdelaine
Porto Torre
Teini · Castel Aragonese
Sassari
C. della Cacca · Cap LUGODORI · C. Comin
Algeri · Gociano · Orose
C. de Bosa
Bosa · Orani
Rade des Salines · SARDAGNE · Guillastro
Oristagni
C. St Marco · Cap CAGLIARI · Mt. Rousse
Villa di Chieza · Cagliari
I. St Pierre · Cap de St Elie · C. Carbonara
I. Sant Lago · Cap Polo
C. de Malfetta
MER · MED · I. de Mare
C. Tavolaro · I. Favg

I. de Minorca

Lieues Comª. de France
5 · 10 · 15 · 20 · 25
10 20 30 40 50 60